PATCHWORK & QUILTING

A MAKER'S GUIDE

With over 210 photographs and illustrations

Thames & Hudson | V&A

First published in the United Kingdom in 2017
by Thames & Hudson in association with the
Victoria and Albert Museum

Patchwork & Quilting: A Maker's Guide
© 2017 Victoria and Albert Museum, London/
Thames & Hudson Ltd, London

V&A images © 2017 Victoria and Albert Museum, London
Illustrations and project photography © 2017 Thames &
Hudson Ltd, London
Text and layout © 2017 Thames & Hudson Ltd, London

See also Picture Credits p.176

Design by Hyperkit
Illustrations by Eleanor Crow
Projects commissioned by Amy Christian
Project editing by Faye Robson
Project photography by We Are Studio

British Library Cataloguing-in-Publication Data

A catalogue record for this book is available from the
British Library

ISBN 978-0-500-29326-3

Printed and bound in China by Toppan Leefung
Printing Limited

To find out about all our publications, please visit
www.thamesandhudson.com. There you can subscribe
to our e-newsletter, browse or download our current
catalogue, and buy any titles that are in print.

Frontispiece: Bed cover (detail), 1800–50
Pieced silk, 231 x 208 cm (91 x 81⅞ in.)
V&A: T.75–1937

Back cover images (clockwise, from top left):
Chunghie Lee, woman's trousers (detail), 1993
Pieced silk gauze, 127 x 44.2 cm (50 x 17⅜ in.)
V&A: FE:281:1-2–1995

Kantha (detail), early 20th century
Embroidered cotton, 89.8 x 86.5 cm (35⅜ x 34 in.)
V&A: IS.16-2008

The 'Tristan' quilt (detail), c.1360–1400
Quilted linen with cotton-wadded trapunto work,
320 x 287 cm (126 x 113 in.)
V&A: 1391–1904

Bed cover (detail), 1860–70
Pieced silk, 79.5 x 40.2 cm (31¼ x 15⅞ in.)
V&A: T.427–1980

Bed cover (detail), 1932
Cotton worked in red cotton thread
V&A: T.134–1932

Mola fragment (detail), mid-20th century
Cotton, 53 x 40 cm (20⅞ x 15¾ in.)
Private collection, courtesy Caroline Crabtree

V&A Publishing

Supporting the world's leading
museum of art and design,
the Victoria and Albert
Museum, London

PATCHWORK & QUILTING TODAY

Andrea Bonfini and Nicola Gomiero founded the experimental fashion brand FADE OUT Label in Berlin in 2015. Their innovative collections are handmade in patchwork using recycled materials.

Both patchwork and quilting are highly popular today and have enjoyed phases of high-end fashionability. Today's globalized and connected society has rediscovered the infinite possibilities of bricolage and is recovering an appreciation of the dexterity and craft that have been eroded by advanced technology and industrial production. While, in the past, it was the scarcity of fabrics that pushed artisans towards creative recycling, today, the abundance (and waste) of raw materials and fabrics awaken critical thinking and push us towards creative recycling as an essential solution.

Both patchwork and quilting techniques developed in ancient times, primarily as ways to recycle and repurpose materials. At various times, the high prices of raw materials and their limited availability have driven communities to invent new solutions for creating fabric for clothing and other purposes: miscellaneous scraps sewn together in a mosaic-like form or stitched together in layers to form a bigger cloth. These composite textiles often reflect their cultures' aesthetic and ethical principles – sobriety, an appreciation of imperfection, and, most importantly, an aversion to waste.

Industrialization made us forget about patched garments and handmade artefacts in the Western world, until they were rediscovered by the avant-garde of early modernism – by artists like Sonia Delaunay. One of the artistic innovations of this period was collage – using diverse materials to create a new surface, in a manner similar to patchworking. At the same time, many everyday materials were adopted as artistic media. Fabric consequently acquired a new value and became part of a theorized artistic language, no longer solely serving to dress and protect the body. These artistic intuitions suggested a new way of living: they re-established a sensorial freshness, reflected in fashions of the period.

In the 1960s, there was a strong critical reaction among young people in the West against overproduction and standardization of consumer products. It wasn't long before street style was adapted to the runway and hippy aesthetics and patchwork entered production chains. But the involved processes of patchwork, especially, were hardly amenable to mechanized production, and so the patchwork trend in fashion was soon represented by printing and pattern, rather than the actual assembly of mixed fabrics.

Today, transforming materials manually for fashion – and not just through patchwork – requires artisans to become completely detached from industrialized fast fashion and to embrace a niche audience of customers who can appreciate the qualities of handcraft and its limited and exclusive availability. At FADE OUT, we have sought to embrace this culture, creating artefacts that reflect an urban, unisex style, using vintage denim and recycled fabrics, patchworked to create simple, original garments. The many hours of manual work needed to create each single item push production to its limits, which is why we choose to offer a permanent collection (see opposite) that does not follow fashion's usual timelines.

It is with great interest that we note the constant evolution of quilting and patchwork as manual art forms with intrinsic potential for innovation. These techniques are stimulating to learn and will allow you to give vent to your own imagination, making unique, personal and ethical creations.

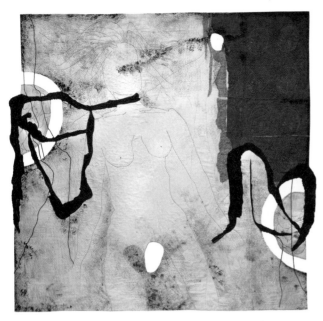

Brigitte Kopp, *Wombs (Gebärmütter)* (textile collage), 2014

FADE OUT Label, 'Ultramarine' blouse from the *Permanent* collection

Kate Loudoun Shand, unique
quilt made for Anthropologie's
New York flagship store, 2011

FADE OUT Label, 'Arctic
Glacier' bomber from the
Volcanoes collection,
Autumn/Winter 2017

Charles James, evening jacket, 1937
V&A: T.385-1977

Schiaparelli, jacket,
Autumn/Winter 2016

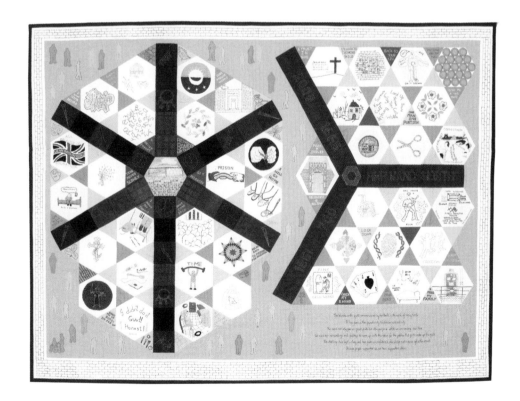

HMP Wandsworth
quilt, created
by the prison's
all-male quilting
group, 2010
V&A: T.27-2010

TOOLS & MATERIALS

Specialist shops and online retailers can provide today's quilter with any number of gadgets and a vast range of fabrics, but you need only a few essential items to get started. In this chapter, we provide information about useful equipment and widely used materials, but each project featured in this book lists the supplies required, so you can check what you need for each one rather than buying everything at once. Make sure you read all project instructions before you start, so you can prepare! The projects featured also mention stitches, some of which may be new to you. Consult the stitch guide on p.17 if you're not familiar with any of the named techniques.

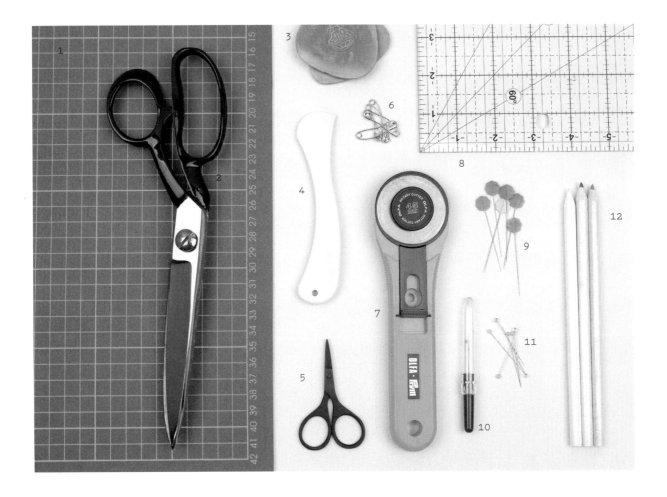

Measuring tools

Tape measure

Choose a good-quality measure made in a material that won't stretch or fray, such as fibreglass. It's useful to have both metric and imperial scales for reference.

Quilting rulers

When cutting out with a rotary cutter (see right), use a thick, acrylic, see-through ruler specially designed for the job (8). Several sizes are available, but the most useful ones are: 6 x 24 in. for cutting strips; 6 x 12 in. for cross-cutting strips and for cutting smaller shapes; and 8 in. or 12 in. square for cutting squares and triangles, and for trimming blocks. You can also buy metric versions.

Markers

A huge range of markers is available, many specifically for fabric. The most commonly used are listed here, but everyone has their favourites, so you may wish to experiment to find which you prefer.

Pencils

A propelling (mechanical) pencil is ideal for drawing around templates and for marking designs onto lighter fabrics, as it allows you to draw accurate lines of a constant width. Quilters' pencils (commonly white or silver; 12) stay sharp and are useful for marking darker fabrics, as are watercolour pencils.

Erasable markers

Air- and water-erasable markers are used for marking lines that you will later want to remove. Air-erasable marks will disappear automatically after a few days so are suitable only for short-term marks. Water-erasable marks are removed by dabbing with a piece of kitchen towel that has been dipped in cold water. Take care if you are pressing, however, as heat can set the marks.

Other markers

Tailor's chalk (3) is quick to use and the marks easily brushed away, but the lines may not be fine enough or sufficiently long-lasting. Hera markers (4) create sharp creases in fabric, which can be useful for marking out straight guidelines. Sometimes a permanent marker is required, perhaps for signing quilt labels. Use a pen that contains archive-quality ink, such as a Pigma pen, as this is resistant to fading.

Cutting tools

Scissors

A pair of dressmaking scissors (2) is required for cutting fabrics (if you are not using a rotary cutter). It's also useful to have a pair of embroidery or sharp, fine-pointed scissors (5) for cutting threads, clipping fabrics and for fine, detailed cutting. Keep a separate pair of scissors for cutting paper and other non-fabrics, as cutting these materials with your fabric or embroidery scissors will ruin the blades. A seam ripper (10) is also useful for unpicking stitching mistakes.

Rotary cutters

These (7) are used in conjunction with a cutting mat and quilting ruler (see column left). They are ideal for cutting long lengths of fabric and basic shapes, and several layers can be cut at once. The most useful size has a 4.5 cm (1¾ in.) blade. There is a variety of handles, so choose one that is comfortable to you. Make sure you cut away from your body and keep your fingers away from the edge of the ruler. The blade is extremely sharp, so always retract and lock it away behind the shield when not using it.

Cutting mats

Used in conjunction with a rotary cutter and quilting ruler, one of these self-healing mats (1) is essential for protecting your work surface. A good basic size is 45.7 x 61 cm (18 x 24 in.) The metric/imperial grids on these mats (usually one on each side) are handy for fabric placement but are not accurate enough for measuring.

Pins

There are a number of different types of pin, but general dressmaking pins are fine for most patchwork and quilting tasks. If you are piecing (joining pieces of fabric) by machine, flat-headed pins (9) are best, as your work will stay flat as you feed it through the machine. If you are working appliqué (applying a fabric motif to the surface of another fabric) or working on fiddly items, small, sharp appliqué pins (11) are useful, as they can be placed close together, and the minimal size of the rounded heads prevents thread from getting caught around them when stitching. Safety pins (6), or curved quilters' safety pins, can be used for pinning quilt layers together (see, for example, pp.47–48).

Note that different fabric glues are available and are an alternative to pins – some provide temporary hold for positioning pieces and others create a permanent bond. For small areas, fabric glue sticks are useful. For small quilts, instead of tacking (basting) or pinning the layers, a basting spray is quick and easy to use; this temporary adhesive can also be used for holding larger fabric pieces in place.

Needles for hand sewing

A wide variety of needles is available, each kind sized and shaped for a different task. Needles also come in different sizes; the higher the number, the smaller and finer the needle. Using the correct needle makes sewing patchwork and quilting easier and more enjoyable.

Sharps

These sharp-pointed needles are for general-purpose sewing, and are also ideal for hand appliqué. It is useful to buy a pack of mixed sizes. For finer fabrics, use a smaller needle.

Embroidery/Crewel

These needles are like sharps, but they have a longer eye so can accommodate thicker threads (17).

Quilting

Also known as 'betweens', these short needles (16) are designed for hand-quilting. The smaller the needle you use, the smaller the stitches you can quilt, but it's best to use a bigger needle (e.g., size 7 or 8) when starting out and to practise working even stitches before worrying about their size.

Hand-quilting tools

A quilting hoop (13), usually wooden, is helpful for supporting a quilt as you work. A popular size is 30.5 cm (12 in.) in diameter. Quilting hoops are deeper than embroidery hoops. The hoop comprises two concentric rings and the quilt is mounted between them, though not pulled taut, or you will find it difficult to stitch through all of the layers.

You need to protect at least the finger pushing the needle through the work and most quilters wear a thimble (14) for this and also on the hand underneath the work. Once you get used to them, wearing thimbles does make stitching easier and quicker. They are available in metal, leather and elastic-type materials.

They also come in a range of styles; as well as a variety of full thimbles there are also open-ended and open-sided versions. You will need to try several on to see which you find most comfortable. If you really don't get on with a thimble, you can buy adhesive finger pads instead.

Machine sewing

A simple machine with basic functions is all that's required for most patchwork and quilting projects. However, a 'needle-down' option is useful as this enables you to set the machine so that when you stop stitching the needle finishes in the work, allowing you to change your sewing direction neatly. A large space between the body of the machine and the needle (the arm length) is also helpful, as it makes it much easier to feed bulkier projects through the machine. If you wish, and especially if your quilt is very large, you can send your finished quilt top to a professional quilter to be quilted on a long-arm machine.

Presser feet

The presser foot keeps the fabric flat and holds it in position against the feed dogs (the teeth that feed fabric through the machine) so that it doesn't move around when sewing. There are specialized feet for different applications. For patchwork and quilting, a good basic selection is: a 6 mm (¼ in.) foot for piecing; a general-purpose foot (18) for straight stitching and narrow zigzag stitch; a walking foot for straight-line quilting; and (especially for the projects included here) a zipper foot (19).

Needles

A variety of needles in a range of sizes is available for sewing with a machine. For general sewing, use a 'universal' needle. For quilting you will need a quilting needle, which has a tapered

point, enabling it to go easily through all the layers of your finished quilt. If stitching with decorative threads, use a machine-embroidery needle, which has a larger eye for ease of threading and a slightly rounded point to prevent damage to thread and fabric.

Fabrics

A vast range of fabrics (20) is available to home crafters (and represented by the projects in this book) – far more than there is room to discuss here. You can always ask at your local haberdashery if you're not sure whether a fabric is suitable for the project you have in mind. The fabric type used in the quilt top is usually also used for a quilt backing.

Quilting cottons

These high-quality, 100% cotton fabrics are available in an extensive range of colours and designs, both solids and prints. Medium-weight dressmaking cottons can also be used for patchwork and quilting, but try to choose firm fabrics with a stiffness similar to that of quilting cottons. Fabrics can be bought 'off the bolt', from rolls that are usually 102–114 cm (40–45 in.) wide, but cuts called fat quarters, which measure 51–57 cm (20–22 in.) wide x 50 cm (19¾ in.) high, are popular. Many manufacturers sell fat quarters and other pre-cut pieces in coordinating bundles, which is useful when building up a fabric collection or if you aren't confident about selecting colours that will work together.

Other fabrics

For wholecloth quilts (which have their tops made from a single piece of fabric; see p.40), cotton silk or cotton sateen give a lovely lustre. For smaller or decorative items, other fabrics can be used, such as silks or wool felts. You can upcycle old jeans or other

21

22

23

24

25

26

27

28

29

garments, but avoid fabrics that are stretchy or thick.

Preparing fabric

Some quilters like to pre-wash their fabrics to pre-shrink them and to check for colour fastness. This isn't usually necessary for decorative items, but sometimes the sizing (the stiffening agent added to fabrics in manufacture) needs to be removed to soften fabric for a larger project.

Threads

An enormous array of threads exists for both hand and machine sewing, with some threads suitable for both. Manufacturers' details will provide the information you need to decide which thread and weight (thickness) best suit your project. The higher a thread weight, the thinner the thread. For fine fabrics, use a thin (high-weight) thread; for thicker fabrics, use a thicker (lower-weight) thread.

General sewing (22)

A 40-weight thread is a popular choice for fabric piecing (by both hand and machine) and appliqué. Most quilters like to use cotton thread with cotton fabrics, but others prefer polyester; it really just comes down to personal choice. For piecing, use a neutral colour that will blend in with your chosen fabrics. For appliqué, use a colour to match the motif fabric.

Tacking (basting)

If tacking quilt layers together, rather than pinning, use proper tacking thread. It breaks easily and doesn't stretch, so it won't damage the fabric or quilted stitches when you remove it from the finished piece.

Quilting

Cotton hand-quilting thread is strong and has a glazed finish. The glazing aids needle threading, helps the thread to glide through the layers of your quilt and prevents tangling. Machine-quilting cottons are unglazed; if using these for hand-quilting, you will need to wax them first. You can also buy 'invisible' nylon thread for machine-quilting – a good choice for beginners.

Decorative and specialist

Threads such as coton à broder, perlé (23) and stranded cottons (floss; 21) can be used to add decorative stitching when hand sewing. For machine work, high-gloss embroidery and metallic threads can be used for quilted and other stitched details.

Wadding (Batting)

The following gives a brief general outline of the most popular waddings – the materials used to 'fill' a quilt.

Natural waddings

The most popular natural waddings are cotton and wool (25–27). Cotton wadding is breathable, so good for bed quilts, but it is fairly low loft (flat). It can be machine- or hand-quilted, but because it's quite firm it's not an easy wadding for beginners to quilt by hand. It becomes softer after each wash (which needs to be done by hand or on a gentle machine cycle). Wool wadding is much softer than cotton and so is a favourite with hand-quilters. Like cotton, it's breathable, but it has a higher loft; it's also beautifully warm and light. Wool quilts need to be washed by hand in cool water.

Synthetic waddings

The most common synthetic wadding is polyester (29), which is light in weight and high in loft. It is suitable for hand- or machine-quilting, but its softness makes it ideal for beginners to hand-quilting. It's also durable and maintains its loft even after repeated machine washing. For a more sustainable option, you can now buy a wadding made from recycled plastic bottles.

Natural/synthetic blends

Cotton/polyester is one of the most widely used waddings, with most blends an 80% cotton/20% polyester mix. It has the look and feel of 100% cotton and is still breathable, but is higher in loft, lighter in weight and able to withstand more frequent washing (28).

General tips and techniques

Units

Both metric and imperial measurements are given in this book. Use one or the other as the sizes are slightly different. This is particularly important for pieced designs such as those in our geometric patchwork chapter (pp.69–117), as mixing units will mean that the fabric pieces will not fit together properly.

Making templates

If you like a particular project in this book and would like to make it again, or re-purpose the design template, you may want to transfer the template onto more durable card or template plastic.

If using template plastic, trace the template/s provided directly onto the plastic with a fine-tipped permanent marker and then cut out neatly. If you are using card, trace the template/s provided onto paper and cut out roughly; glue onto card (cereal packets are ideal) and then cut out neatly along the drawn line. If you want to 'fussy cut' your fabric pieces (see 'English paper piecing' on pp.84–91, for example) a window template is useful. To make a window template, trace the template itself and then add a 6 mm (¼ in.) seam allowance all around. Cut along both lines to leave a 6 mm frame. When you place this template on fabric you will be able to view how the finished piece will look.

Cutting out

Woven fabric has two straight grains. The crosswise grain runs widthwise, from selvedge to selvedge, and the lengthwise grain runs parallel to the selvedges. Straight-grain edges are the most stable so, wherever possible, cut your fabric pieces so that seams are on a straight grain. The bias is a diagonal grain, with the true bias at 45 degrees to the straight grains. Bias edges are stretchy and tend to distort. If working with bias edges, e.g. triangle or diamond shapes, you can use spray starch to help stabilize the edges. Do not include fabric selvedges in your quilt, as these are usually more tightly woven than the fabric. Before cutting out, press your fabrics well.

Cutting out with templates: Place the template against the wrong side of the fabric, hold it still and then draw around it carefully with a fine marker before cutting.

Cutting out with a rotary cutter: Rotary cutters are used in conjunction with a cutting mat and quilting ruler. Before cutting strips, you need to straighten the fabric. If you are working with width-of-fabric pieces, the fabric will need to be folded selvedge to selvedge before cutting, so take care to ensure that both the crosswise and lengthwise grains are aligned. If you are going to cut width-of-fabric strips, then leave the fabric folded. If you are cutting several strips from a piece of fabric, after a few strips you might need to re-straighten it.

To cut a strip, align your ruler at the desired width from the straightened edge. It's important to be accurate, so check the placement of your ruler along the entire length to make sure it's straight.

Strips are the basis for cutting several patchwork shapes. Strips can be cross-cut into squares and rectangles, and these can be sub-cut further to make triangles.

Piecing

The standard seam allowance for patchwork is 6 mm (¼ in.), but check the instructions for the project you're working on, as they may vary. As with cutting out, it's important to be accurate. When multiplied by all the seams in a quilt top, even small differences can introduce significant variation in sizes, which makes a quilt difficult to piece neatly.

Hand piecing: When joining pieces by hand, mark the seam with a pencil or fabric marker on the wrong side of one of the pieces being joined (usually the lighter fabric). Place the pieces right sides together and pin to secure. Sew along the marked line with a small running stitch, starting and stopping 6 mm (¼ in.) from each end of the seam, i.e., do not sew through the seam intersection. You can start and end with a knot or a few backstitches.

Machine piecing: Before you start, make sure your machine is set to sew a 6 mm (¼ in.) seam and, if you have one, place the 6 mm (¼in.) presser foot on your machine. Place the pieces to be joined right sides together and sew the whole length of the seam. There is no need to mark or pin the seam, or to take backstitches at either end. Press the seam to one side with an iron, usually towards the darker fabric.

Transferring designs

Where a project instructs you to transfer a design onto the background fabric or quilt top, use one of the methods given here as appropriate. Note that for quilts, quilting designs are transferred to the right side of the quilt top before it is layered with the wadding and backing fabric.

Tracing: First, trace the design template provided onto tracing or white paper using a permanent marker (you may need to photocopy or otherwise enlarge the design before you do this, so check the relevant project instructions). Use as fine a tip as you can, while ensuring that the lines are bold enough to show through the fabric. For light materials you might be able to see the design through the fabric when both are placed on a worktop, but if not, and for darker fabrics, you will need to hold both paper and fabric up to a window or lightbox.

If using a window, tape the traced design to a window and then tape the fabric over the top (use either masking or adhesive tape). Make sure the fabric is taut and positioned correctly. Trace the design using the marker recommended for the project you are making.

For dark fabrics, or when designs can't be traced directly, dressmaker's carbon paper can be used. First trace the design provided onto tracing or white paper, as above. Place the dressmaker's carbon paper carbon-side down onto the right side of the fabric and then place the traced design on top of it (you can hold the papers in place with pins). Draw over the lines of the design with a pencil or ballpoint pen to transfer the design. This method is best suited to smaller projects, as the paper can move around, making it difficult to trace smooth lines.

STITCH GUIDE

Refer to this step-by-step guide when you
come across unfamiliar stitches. It may
be a good idea to practise a new stitch
on a piece of scrap fabric first.

Running stitch

Bring the thread up through
the fabric at 1, down at
2 (working right to left),
up at 3, down at 4 and so on.
Length of stitches and spaces
can be varied for different
effects. Tacking (basting)
stitches are extra long
running stitches.

Backstitch

Bring the thread up through
the fabric at 1 and back down
at 2 (working right to left).
Bring it up again at 3, then
back down at 1, and so on.
Aim for a continuous line
of stitches with no gaps.
Make shorter stitches for
curved lines.

Slip stitch

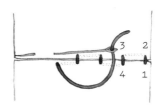

Bring the thread up through
the fabric at 1 and over
to 2 (working from right
to left). Take it over to 3,
keeping the thread under the
fabric. Go down again at 4,
and so on. Only the vertical
stitches should be visible.

Whip stitch

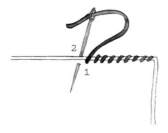

To join layered fabrics,
bring the thread up through
both pieces of fabric at 1
and again at 2 (working from
right to left). Stitches
should be small and close
together.

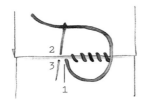

To whip stitch a seam, bring
the thread up through the
bottom piece of fabric at 1.
Insert it into all layers
at 2, and back through the
bottom piece at 3 (slightly
to the left of your starting
point). Bring the thread
through and continue to work
from right to left.

Blanket/Buttonhole
stitch

Take the thread down through
the fabric at 1 and up at
2 (working left to right),
keeping thread looped under
the needle. Pull the thread
through. For buttonhole
stitch, work stitches closer
together.

RUNNING-STITCH QUILTING

As far as we know, the earliest quilted work consisted of two outer layers of fabric with a layer of padding in between. These layers were probably evenly and methodically sewn together to form a new fabric, with the stitching creating a decoration; where two layers of fabric are stitched together with an elaborate, all-over pattern, this too forms a type of quilting. The stitching in all types of quilting, up to the present day, is consistent – running stitch and backstitch are the usual methods and form the basis of regional techniques ranging from English and Welsh wholecloth and 'strippy' quilting (see pp.40–49), to Japanese *sashiko* (see pp.20–29) and a myriad of traditions from the Indian subcontinent: Pakistani *ralli* and *kanbiri*; Banjara textiles from Rajasthan and the patterns of Indian *kantha* (see pp.30–39).

Coverlet, early 20th century
Quilted and embroidered cotton, 98 x 79 cm (38½ x 31⅛ in.)
V&A: IS.4–2011

SASHIKO

The word *sashiko* is derived from *sasu*, meaning 'to pierce or prick', with the suffix *ko* meaning 'small'. The technique of *sashiko* is simply one of running stitches sewn through layers of fabric (typically white cotton thread, worked through indigo-dyed cotton or hemp), creating a variety of geometric patterns. While the technique has been in existence in Japan since at least the eighth century, primarily as a form of advanced darning and patching – intended to extend the life and improve the insulating properties and durability of textiles – it began to be practised for its decorative value from the eighteenth and nineteenth centuries, with newly available, highly contrasting cotton thread used with traditional, indigo-dyed fabrics.

Meaningful design

Sashiko stitching creates often quite complex geometric patterns from straight lines intersecting at right angles. Sometimes, these take the form of stylized and abstracted natural motifs – for example, in the case of the classic *kakinohanazashi* (persimmon flower) or *asanoha* (hemp leaf) patterns. The patterns are repetitive and based on a grid of vertical and horizontal (and, sometimes, diagonal) lines; this complex array of stitches makes *sashiko* strong and well suited to the workwear and functional textiles for which the technique was originally used. The *asanoha* pattern is frequently sewn into infant clothing and bedding.

Jacket, late 19th-early 20th century
Quilted cotton with paste-resist decoration,
95 x 122 cm (37⅜ x 48 in.)
V&A: FE.107-1982

Sledge-Hauling Jacket, late 19th century

The diagonal band across this jacket was intended to reinforce the garment against the rubbing of sledge-hauling ropes. Made of blue cotton and 14 cm (5½ in.) wide, it has been quilted in double, white cotton thread in a concentric diamond design known as the *kakinohanazashi* or persimmon flower pattern (another similar band is sewn over the right shoulder); this pattern inspired the project overleaf. The *sashiko* stitching continues – in dark-blue thread against a blue ground – across the main body of the garment, with three distinct patterns used to both decorate and reinforce the two layers of indigo-dyed cotton fabric that make up the body of the garment.

Quilted cotton, 83 x 57.5 cm (32⅝ x 22⅝ in.)
V&A: FE.108–1982

SHONAI SASHIKO TABLE RUNNER

Kakinohanazashi (persimmon flower stitch) is combined with a *kamon* (family crest) motif from a Japanese *noren* (door curtain) in this table runner design. Using a traditional indigo-and-white colour scheme, it is stitched through a single length of fabric (*sashiko* can, traditionally, be sewn through any number of layers, but this is a good way to practise the technique before taking on projects with multiple layers; see pp.136–41). The only stitch used is **running stitch** (see p.17) and the table runner may be made to your desired length.

You will need

Dark-blue cotton fabric, 133 x 37 cm (52¼ x 14¾ in.), or a size of your choice

One 100 m skein *sashiko* thread, Olympus medium, cream or white (see notes on *sashiko* fabric and thread, p.28)

General sewing thread, to match *sashiko* fabric

Sashiko needle, suitable for medium *sashiko* thread

Hand-sewing needle

Dressmaker's carbon paper or Japanese *chaco* (chalk transfer) paper

Quilting rulers: ideally, metric and imperial

Erasable marker, suitable for dark fabrics

Pen or pencil

Optional

Dark backing fabric, 133 x 37 cm (52¼ x 14¾ in.), or to match your table runner

Tracing paper

Project by Susan Briscoe

How to make

1 Begin by marking the area of persimmon flower stitch (for the ends of the runner). Use an erasable marker and quilting rulers to mark a grid for the stitch. (This style of *sashiko* – *hitomesashi* (one stitch) – used to be stitched without marking, but nowadays a grid is usually marked). The 'flowers' in this pattern are slightly elongated, so the lines running across and along the fabric must be spaced differently. Draw eleven parallel lines across the width of the fabric, starting 9 cm (3½ in.) from each short end, with the lines spaced 6 mm (¼ in.) apart. Starting and finishing 1 cm (⅜ in.) from each long side of the fabric, draw another set of parallel lines crossing these, to form a grid, with the lines spaced 5 mm (³⁄₁₆ in.) apart. Mark as many lines as needed to fill the width of the fabric. It is easier to mark the 6 mm (¼ in.) lines using an imperial ruler, and the 5 mm (³⁄₁₆ in.) lines with a metric ruler.

2 Thread your *sashiko* needle with a whole length of thread, approximately 1 m (40 in.) long, and double it by bringing the ends together. Smooth the thread, so it doesn't twist around itself, and tie a single knot at the end. The thread now can't fall out of your needle if you drop it! A doubled thread is traditional in *sashiko*. Start and finish stitching with a single knot on the reverse of the work. Join new threads with a *hatamusubi* (weaver's knot), for complete authenticity, as shown opposite.

3 Now work your persimmon flower stitch. There are two stages to working the stitch on your grid – first horizontally, then vertically – and a pattern is created where the two sets of stitches meet. Stitch back and forth across the width of the fabric first, going up and down through the fabric where the drawn grid lines intersect, as shown in the illustration right. Note that the diagrams show a small area of the pattern rather than the full fabric width; the red and black lines are just there to aid you in following the pattern – you don't need different threads! Note also that there are no 'double' gaps in the pattern.

Tip: *You are aiming for nice fat running stitches (see p.17), where the two threads lie parallel, slightly raised from the fabric surface. Keep sewing straight and even by making several stitches with the needle before pulling the thread through, gathering the fabric up slightly and easing the gathers out along the thread as you go. This stitching action keeps the threads parallel in the stitch. Leave a little loop for ease when turning at the end of each row, to stop your work pulling in.*

Start here

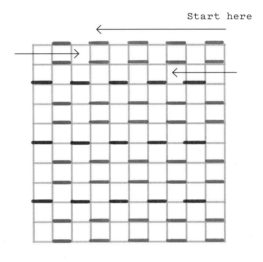

Start here

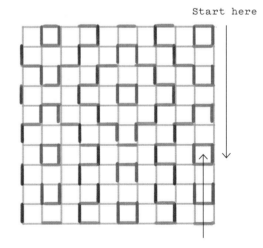

The *Hatamusubi* (Weaver's Knot)

  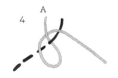 

1 Leave a 2.5 cm (1 in.) tail of your old thread, shown in black here, loose on the back of the work. Thread the *sashiko* needle with, but do not knot, your new thread. Lay the ends of the new thread (shown in yellow) against the back of the work.

2 Hold the end of the new thread between your index and middle fingers on your left hand (at point A), wedging the fabric between your other fingers. Use your left thumb to bend the tail of the old thread over the new. Put your thumb on the crossed threads to hold them in place until instructed otherwise.

3 Now the long part of the new thread does most of the work. Loop it to the left, as shown here. Lift your thumb quickly, pass the thread under it and hold the crossed threads again.

4 Now take the long part of the new thread under its own tail and over the old thread – the new thread should have made a loop. Continue to hold the thread with your fingers at point A.

5 Now use your left thumb to bend the old thread tail through the loop you just made and hold the end between your left thumb and left ring finger at point B. Holding the two short ends so they can't flip out of the knot, pull on the long new thread gently, with your right hand, to tighten the knot and pull it closed.

Once the persimmon flower stitch has been worked, the runner can be hemmed, as per step 5.

4 Once the first eleven horizontal rows of the pattern have been worked, begin sewing the shorter, vertical rows, as shown in the illustration opposite below, starting at one side of the fabric and working across. You do not need to go up and down through the fabric at the exact same point as the previous stitches so long as the ends of your stitches are very close.

5 Press and hem the ends of the runner. First, fold over 1 cm (⅜ in.) at each end of the runner and press towards the back of the work. Fold again so that blank fabric covers the back of all the persimmon flower stitches, and use a **whip stitch** (see p.17) to secure the fold. Sew up the sides of this wide hem with tiny running stitches, to close the gap.

6 Photocopy or trace the *tachibana* (orange blossom) *kamon* crest opposite, and transfer the full-size design to the centre of your table runner. Start by finding the centre point of your runner, by folding it in half in both directions. You can now position and transfer the design to your runner, using either an erasable marker and lightbox or window (see p.16), or Japanese *chaco* paper/dressmaker's carbon paper. If using *chaco* paper, place the design template over the *sashiko* fabric and pin in place. Slide the *chaco* paper under the template, coloured side up, and, on a hard surface, trace around the diagram lines using a ballpoint pen. Check that the design has transferred and that you have gone over all the lines on the diagram before removing pins.

Notes on *sashiko*

Fabric

Sashiko is most often traditionally stitched on indigo-coloured fabrics. Shonai *sashiko*, from Yamagata prefecture in Japan, is typically stitched on a very dark blue, as this was the most expensive indigo fabric available and showed a family's wealth. The narrow cotton used for traditional farmers' clothing in Shonai was used for our table runner, with the selvedges left in place; the runner is hemmed only at the short ends. If you are using a wider fabric, backing the finished table runner with another piece of cotton may give a more attractive finish than hemming the piece all round (see step 8).

Thread

A skein of *sashiko* thread is packaged in such a way that it won't unravel direct from the skein. Remove the paper band, cut through the skein where all the threads are tied together, and loosely plait the threads to stop them tangling. Don't worry if you cannot get *sashiko* thread: you can use coton à broder or perlé cotton instead.

7 Stitch *sashiko* over the design template, using running stitches 3 mm (⅛ in.) in length, with gaps half the length of the stitches. Work around the central 'flower' first, followed by the leaves around the flower and, finally, the lower leaves and stem. **Note:** *The stitches do not cross where the motif lines cross – leave a little gap so that the stitches cross on the back of your work rather than the front. When you make a sharp change of direction, leave a little loop on the back for ease or the sashiko will pucker. Press to finish.*

8 If you wish, you can back the runner rather than hemming it. Do this using the 'bagging out' method, i.e., place your fabric backing (which should be the same size as your *sashiko* panel) and stitched panel right sides together, and stitch around the entire edge using a 1 cm (⅜ in.) seam allowance. Leave a 10 cm (4 in.) gap unsewn on one long edge. **Note:** *If you do this, you do not need to hem the short ends of the runner, as instructed in step 5.* Now make a couple of snips into the seam allowance at each corner, cutting close to, but not through, the seam, and turn the whole right side out through the unsewn gap. Press and use a **slip stitch** (see p.17) to close up the unsewn gap. For a very crisp finished edge, sew small, invisible running stitches all around the runner from the back, catching the seam allowance 3 mm (⅛ in.) from the edge but without letting your stitching show through on the front of the work.

Now try...

Adapting these stitch patterns and designs for a larger runner, or for table mats. The latter are a good opportunity to practise working *sashiko* through multiple layers. A thin wadding (batting) can be tacked (basted) to your sewn *sashiko* panel before the backing is sewn on (see step 8), and extra quilting worked through the whole after it has been turned right side out.

Design template

Template shown at 100%

KANTHA

Aesthetically related to, in particular, the Banjara textile tradition of the Indian subcontinent — which is often characterized by quilting executed in off-white thread, afterwards embellished with contrast-coloured thread woven through the surface stitching in bold geometric designs — *kantha* stitching takes the principle of quilting with embroidery further. Traditionally an example of 'flat', or unwadded, quilting, a Bangladeshi or Bengali *kantha* cloth is worked on multiple layers of fabric. The stitching consists of embroidered patterns, ranging from simple floral motifs to elaborate scenes, combined with running-stitch quilting in a colour matching the background fabric. On older quilts, the quilting runs around the embroidered motifs, a technique known as echo quilting.

Make do and mend

In the past, making *kanthas* was very much a craft born of recycling; the layers of fabric were made from old, worn sari lengths, softened by wear and washing. Coloured threads were pulled from the sari borders to be reused in the decorative stitching. The fact that the saris were well used meant that all fabric and threads were colour-fast and unlikely to fade any more than they already had. Today, *kantha*-making using new fabric has been embraced by a number of projects aimed at preserving traditional skills and generating income for the women of poorer communities. Today, the word *kantha* is more often used as a description of a stitching style than the object. As with *sashiko* for Japan, the *kantha* style is now regarded with pride as a symbol of Bangladeshi culture.

Kantha, early 20th century
Embroidered cotton, 89.8 x 86.5 cm
(35⅜ x 34 in.)
V&A: IS.16-2008

Kantha, 1900–50

This small, rectangular coverlet is made up of layers of cotton, with the uppermost undyed and providing a simple backdrop to the bold motifs embroidered in red, blue and yellow. The colours have been placed carefully and increase the impact of the relatively simple decorative designs – flowers, spirals and paisley motifs. *Kantha* designs are not always so geometrical or regular, as is evidenced by other items in the Victoria and Albert Museum collection, including a brightly coloured sitting mat decorated with scenes of human figures, Hindu deities, animals and plants (see previous page).

Quilted and embroidered cotton, 80 x 69 cm (31½ x 27⅛ in.)
V&A: IS.6-2011

TABLET OR PHONE SLEEVE

Kantha were originally made from old sari lengths, the fabric worn soft through repeated washings and therefore particularly suitable for wrapping cloths or baby quilts. The idea of a soft, layered, but durable cloth has inspired this sleeve for your tablet or phone. The (adaptable) instructions given here will create a snug fit for your chosen object – you can add a little more ease if you wish.

You will need

Lightweight calico (unbleached cotton cloth; go for something similar to cheesecloth, as normal-weight calico is too thick and stiff), 50 cm (20 in.) should be sufficient for most projects, assuming cut to width of fabric

Brushed-cotton fabric in white or cream, the same size as the calico

Thread, DMC Broder Special, no. 25: two skeins each of 304 (cherry red), 322 (mid blue) and 823 (dark blue), and one skein each of 902 (dark red) and 3865 (ivory)

General sewing thread, to match calico

Hand-sewing needle

Tape measure

Tracing paper

Pen or pencil

Water-erasable marker

Pins

Optional

Sewing machine and related threads

Project by Caroline Crabtree

How to make

1 Prepare your materials (see p.15). Lightweight calico must be washed at 90°C (194°F) to remove dressing and soften the fabric.

2 Photocopy or otherwise enlarge the design template on p.39 to full size, i.e. 100%.

3 Work out the area of the design template needed for your project (the full template provided will fit a tablet 24 x 17 cm (9½ x 6¾ in.); you will only need a section of the design for a smaller gadget). Measure the 'circumference' of your gadget (i.e. wrap the tape measure around it widthwise) and add 3 cm (1¼ in.); this is your 'width'. Measure again lengthwise, halve this number and add 2.5 cm (1 in.); this is your 'length'. Draw this area onto tracing paper and place over the full-size design template to decide which section to use. Trace off the design. **Tip:** *As the embroidery is almost reversible (if one finishes threads neatly) the case is not lined. If you want to add a lining, you will need to make the stitched section larger – add about 1 cm (⅜ in.) to each measurement.*

4 Add 8 cm (3¼ in.) to both your length and width measurements. Cut two pieces of calico and one piece of brushed cotton to this size. Placing one piece of calico over your traced design, you should be able to trace the design onto the fabric directly, using a water-erasable marker.

5 Place the brushed cotton between the two calico pieces, with the calico piece featuring the traced design uppermost. Pin or tack (baste) the layers together.

6 Work your stitching through all three layers, starting with the straight lines, which should be worked with a double row of **running stitch** (see p.17; this double-row technique gives the characteristic, slightly wavy outline of traditional *kantha*). Work one row first, and then the second, placing stitches in the gaps made by the first row. Stitch the outline of the petalled flower shapes, including the centres, in the same way. You can position colours as you choose, or follow the photographs here.

7 Fill the petals by, first, working a double row of running stitch around the inner outline of each petal. Now work rows of running stitch from this line outwards, creating 'bars' of stitching. **Tip:** *Work backwards and forwards around the shape – don't work one bar to the edge and then move on to the next. Stop halfway out and then work back in towards the centre from the outer outline, making bars in the spaces left by the previous stitches.*

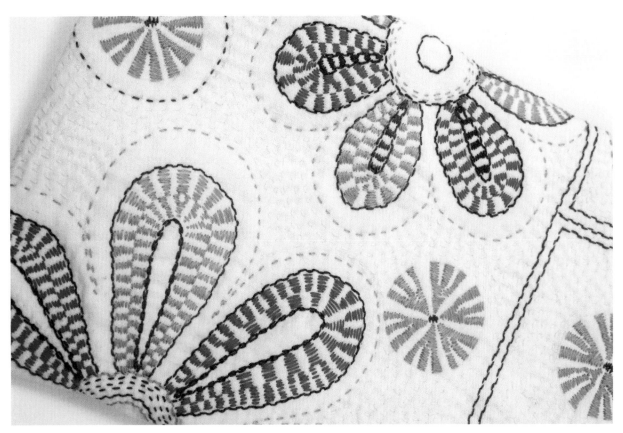

Work stitching in the order directed by steps 6-11.

8 The centre spaces in the smaller flower petals can also be filled with running stitch; work from the centre of the flower outwards.

9 The smaller, 'cartwheel' flowers are worked as follows: first, make a row of running stitch around the outer edge of the shape (two or three stitches per segment). Now work rows of running stitch inwards, towards the centre of the flower, again creating bars. When the stitches and spaces between them become too small, you can combine two or three bars into one (see photo above).

10 To finish, work a single row of running stitch around the larger flowers, and some of the small cartwheel flowers, approx. 1.2 cm (½ in.) from the flower outline. Work two or three rows of single running stitch inside the large flower centres. Make small centres in the cartwheel flowers, by making a cluster of small, straight stitches.

11 Using the ivory-coloured thread (3865), work single rows of running stitch around the contours of the design, with the rows approx. 3 mm (⅛ in.) apart. If necessary, remove any visible pen marks (see p.11).

12 Cut two more pieces from the calico: one 40 x 5 cm (15¾ x 2 in.), for the ties, and one piece measuring the width of your quilted panel x 10 cm (4 in.)

13 Make up the ties by folding the first piece of calico in half, lengthwise, right sides together. **Backstitch** (see p.17) or machine sew together along the long raw edges using a 6 mm (¼ in.) seam. Turn the tube right side out and cut in half, to give two ties. **Note:** *The short ends are left raw.*

14 Fold your quilted panel in half widthwise, wrong sides together. Pin a tie at the centre of each top edge of the sleeve, so the ties are opposite each other, allowing for the side seam (see step 16). Re-open the panel and lay it flat, right side up.

15 Fold your second calico piece in half lengthwise. Matching up all raw edges, place this calico strip along the top edge of the quilted panel. The ties will be sandwiched between the two. Stitch along the top edge using a 1 cm (⅜ in.) seam allowance; this will also secure the ties in place.

16 Press the calico strip upwards, away from the quilted panel. Fold the whole assembly in half widthwise, right sides together. Stitch the side and base seam using a 1 cm (⅜ in.) seam allowance, pivoting at the corner.

17 Trim seam allowances to 6 mm (¼ in.) with the brushed cotton trimmed further, as tight to the stitching as possible. Neaten the seam allowance using pinking shears or a zigzag (machine) stitch to neaten and prevent fraying.

18 Fold the calico strip back down, so that it makes a facing on the inside of the open (top) sleeve edge. Press and **slip stitch** (see p.17) the edge of the facing down.

19 Make a knot at the end of each tie, so that the raw end is caught inside the knot as much as possible. Turn the sleeve right side out to finish.

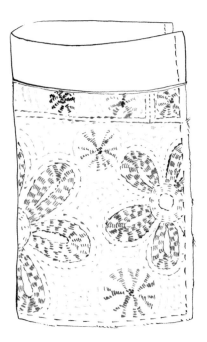

Now try...

Scaling up. The *kantha*-stitched fabric is soft, hard-wearing and reversible. It is also easily laundered, making it ideal for a baby's quilt. Experiment with the individual motifs provided to create your own, larger design.

Design template

Template shown at 50%

Will fit a tablet
24 x 17 cm (9½ x 6¾ in.)

Will fit a mini tablet
20 x 13.5 cm (8 x 5¼ in.)

WHOLECLOTH

In nineteenth-century Britain, quilting was widely practised in rural areas, distant from the influence of London. Two very different strands of 'quilt' making, broadly speaking, existed: the work of genteel ladies who were stitching mosaic patchwork or embellished coverlets (which were not necessarily actually quilted); and the wholecloth or pieced medallion-style quilts (dominated by a central area or motif), which were wadded and quilted, usually in a limited colour palette. These two forms had inevitable class associations. In schools, young girls were taught embroidery, paper piecing (see pp.80-91), and appliqué – the 'socially acceptable' forms of needlework – but they were not taught traditional quilting. Today, wholecloth quilting in particular has enjoyed a resurgence, with elaborate quilting patterns and even pre-marked quilt tops available to buy.

North Country and Welsh Quilting

Quilting in the north of England was an essential part of the rural economy; many experienced quilters lacked the confidence to design quilting patterns for themselves, however, so it was the custom to send the tops to a professional marker, who drew designs onto the cloth. Renowned markers and designers include Joseph Hedley and George Gardiner, whose apprentice, Elizabeth Sanderson, became even better known.

In Wales, quilting was also an integral part of rural and mining communities; the Welsh had itinerant quilters, however, who travelled from farm to farm. While both traditions included wholecloth, 'strippy' (strip-pieced) and pieced medallion quilts, differences include the Welsh preference for using woollen wadding (batting) and fabrics over cotton, as well as a broad tendency to favour strong lines and bold colours, like those seen in North American Amish quilts (see pp.92-93).

English cot cover, 1750-1800
Quilted satin-weave silk and linen
with wool wadding, 115 x 87 cm
(45¼ x 34¼ in.)
V&A: T.429-1966

Bed cover, c.1900

Believed to have been made in Northumberland, England, this medallion-style bed cover has been pieced in pale- and bright-yellow cotton sateen and quilted all over with a design based on the popular 'Sanderson Star', which was originally developed by the professional quilter Elizabeth Sanderson. This quilt testifies to her significance as a designer, and her ongoing influence, due in no small part to her role as a teacher of professional quilting apprentices. Girls would train with her for a period of six months to a year, at the end of which they might be taken on as professional quilt markers.

Quilted cotton sateen, 233 x 210 cm (91¾ x 82⅝ in.)
V&A: T.255–1979

NORTH COUNTRY COT QUILT

This is a traditional North Country cot quilt design; there is no patching or appliqué involved, just hand-quilting, which creates lovely patterns and textures. If you use different colours for the front and back, the quilt will be completely reversible.

You will need

Cotton or cotton-silk mix in a plain colour, 1 m (1 yd) for the quilt top and 1 m (1 yd) for the quilt backing (it's up to you whether these are matching or not)

Wadding (batting) (see p.15), dimensions as above

Tacking (basting) thread

Hand-quilting thread, to match top fabric

Hand-sewing needle

Quilting needle, size 9 or 10

Tracing paper

Bold- (broad-)nib permanent marker pen

Water-erasable marker, quilting pencil or dressmaker's chalk

Safety pins or quilters' safety pins

Embroidery, or other sharp, fine-pointed scissors

Optional

Quilting hoop

Thimble (see p.12)

Quilters' ¼ in.-wide tape

Project by Pippa Moss. Finished dimensions: 66 x 100 cm (26 x 39¾ in.)

How to make

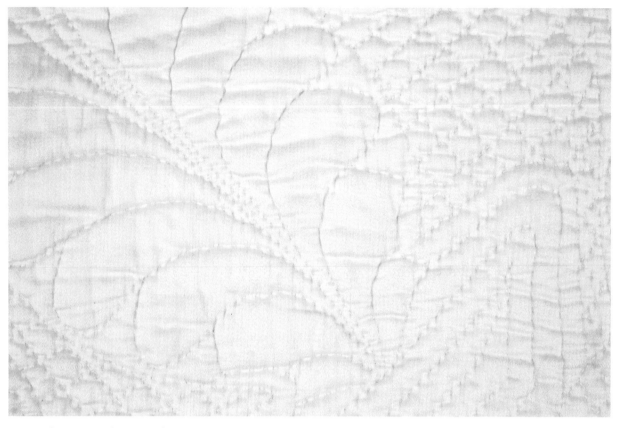

Hand-quilt the designs, as instructed in step 9 and 'Hand-quilting' (p.48).

1 Take your top fabric; fold in half lengthwise and press. Now fold in half widthwise, carefully matching the edges and folds, and press again. Leave the fabric folded. The pressed creases provide guidelines for marking the quarter-pattern onto the fabric (see steps 4 and 5). The quilt is not cut to size until after all stitching has been worked, but do make sure you have removed any selvedges before you start working (see p.16).

2 Photocopy or otherwise enlarge the quilting design on p.49 to full size, i.e. 100%.

3 Trace the quilting design template onto tracing paper using the marker, so that it will be visible through your top fabric.

4 For light-coloured fabrics: unfold your fabric and slide your quarter-pattern under one quarter of the top fabric, matching up the pressed creases with the dashed-line edges of the quarter pattern. Pin or tape the pattern and fabric in place to avoid movement and trace the pattern onto your fabric using an erasable marker. For darker fabrics, you may have to first tape the pattern to a lightbox or window, tape the fabric in place and trace using a white quilting pencil or dressmaker's chalk, for contrast (see p.16 for complete instructions).

5 Mark the other three quarters of the pattern in the same fashion, rotating and flipping the pattern as necessary.

6 Once the larger pattern motifs are marked, you can fill the background with cross-hatching. Use the diagonal of the pattern, from one corner across to the other, to mark the first line and then mark lines parallel to this one at 1 cm (3/8 in.) intervals. Do the same working in the opposite direction. If you prefer, you could use quilters' 1/4 in.-wide tape to mark your diagonal lines; this purpose-designed, lightly adhesive tape will leave no residue on your fabric.

7 Once the pattern has been marked, layer the quilt top for quilting. Lay your backing fabric, right side down, on a flat surface. Lay your wadding (batting) on top and smooth out any wrinkles. Lay the marked top, right side up, over both layers and smooth again.

8 Pin or tack the layers together, to avoid movement while the layers are quilted. Tacking (basting) stitches can be run parallel to the quilt edges in a vertical and horizontal grid, or in a spider's web, running from the centre outwards; they should be 5-8 cm (2-3 in.) apart, so that the whole is firmly held together.

9 Hand-quilt the marked designs, using a quilting needle and matching thread (see p.48). Quilting proceeds from the centre, outwards to the edges of the quilt. Keep the fabric smooth (using a quilting hoop, if you wish) and be careful not to rub off the quilting designs as you work. Once the quilting is complete, if necessary, remove any visible pen marks (see p.11).

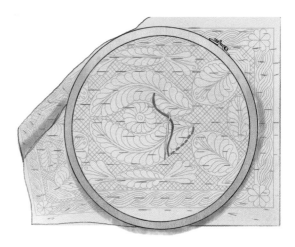

Hand-quilting

Start by cutting a piece of quilting thread approx. 46 cm (18⅛ in.) long and threading your needle with a long 'tail'. Knot the end of your thread and pass the needle into the top fabric, approx. 2 cm (¾ in.) away from where you want to start quilting. Pass the needle through the wadding and back to the surface – a slight tug on the tread will 'pop' the knot into the wadding and hide it.

Hand-quilting stitch is really only a **running stitch** (see p.17), where two or more stitches are picked up onto the needle at once, before the needle is pulled through. The hand with the needle remains above the quilt, while the other hand remains below, feeling for the end of the needle and helping to push it back to the surface. Practise making a single stitch, then try 'rocking' the needle up and down through the fabric to pick up more stitches before drawing the needle through – this is quicker and helps to make your stitches more even. **Tips:** *6–8 stitches every 2.5 cm (1 in.) is great. It may help to use a thimble on top of the quilt, as it will stop the sharp needle from hurting your fingers and will help you to achieve this rocking stitch.*

If you are lap quilting (working without a quilting hoop), the technique is slightly different. Hold the quilt sandwich between the thumb and fingers of your non-needle hand and, using both hands, feed the tensioned fabric onto the needle by moving it backwards and forwards, while pushing the needle forwards. Watch your thread tension – you must avoid pulling the thread too tight, or you will get an odd, puckered effect.

When you get near the end of the thread, put another knot on the surface of the quilt. Put the needle back down through the last needle hole and emerge through the layers further away. Pulling on the tail of the thread will 'pop' the knot under the quilt top and secure it. You can trim the thread, then rethread your needle and start quilting again.

10 Use a traditional knife-edge binding to finish your quilt. Trim the quilt layers to 2.5 cm (1 in.) beyond the quilted area. Trim the wadding back a further 6 mm (¼ in.). Now turn and press the edges of the quilt top and backing under by approx. 6 mm (¼ in.), squaring the corners. Pin, matching up the neatened edges, and then work a **running stitch** (see p.17) close to the neatened edge. Sew another line approx. 1.3 cm (½ in.) in from the first line of stitching.

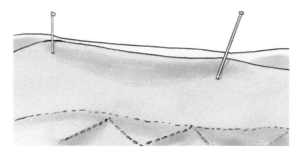

11 Wash the quilt with a gentle detergent and label with your name, date and any other wording you wish.

Now try...

Different templates. It is possible to make your own quilting templates from designs in books and magazines, or even from the internet. Simply photocopy the designs (you can enlarge or decrease the size) and glue to card or template plastic. Cut around the outside and you have a sturdy template for repeat use.

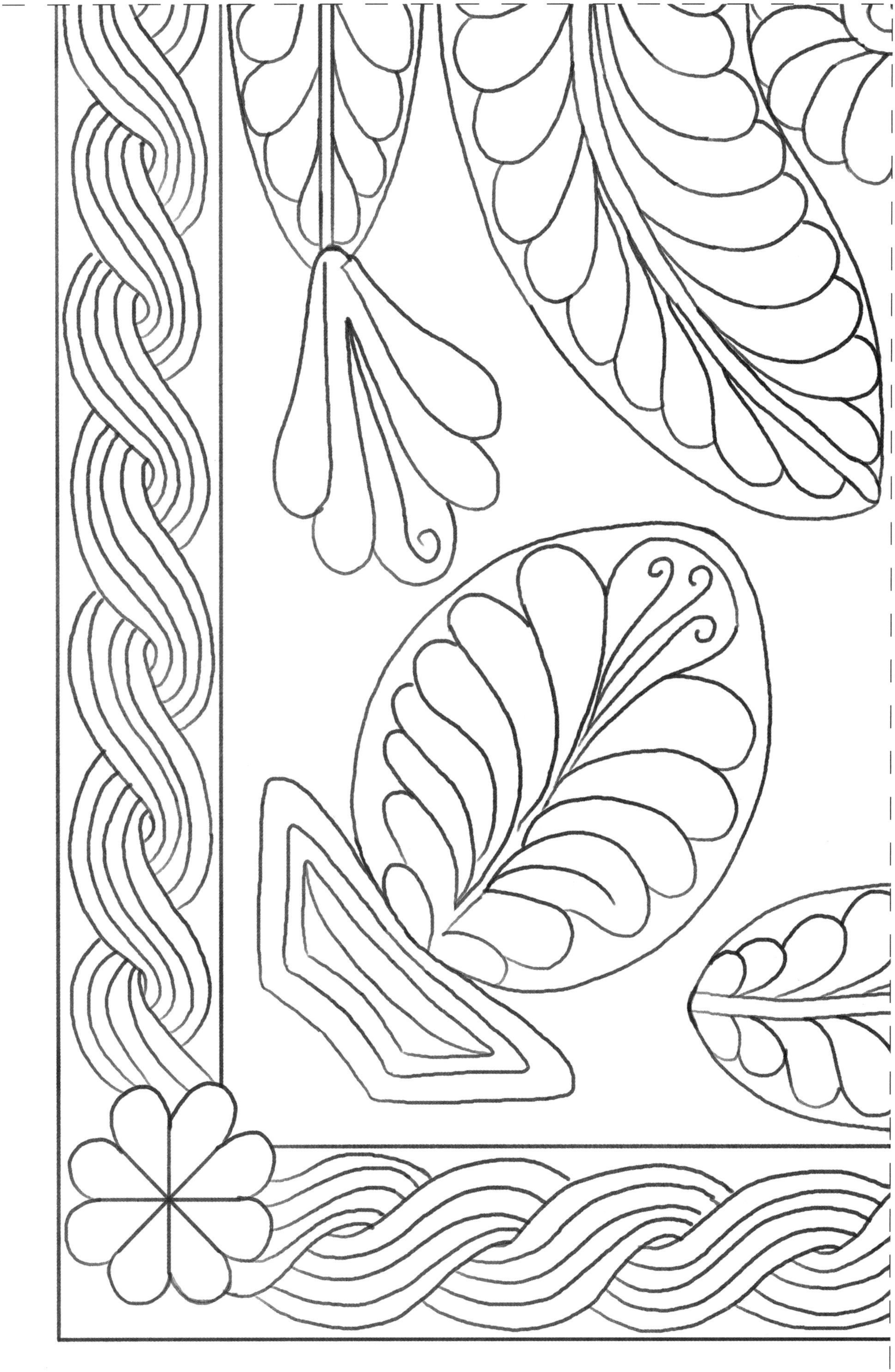

Quilting design template

Template shown at 50%

STUFFED —— & PADDED QUILTING

Alongside basic quilting techniques, which developed worldwide, a different kind of work emerged: this has a raised pattern created by the insertion of a cord or padding. This is somewhat different to 'wadded' quilting (of which wholecloth and Amish quilts are familiar examples) in which a thicker, more substantial layer has been added to the body of a quilt, usually for added warmth. While wadded quilting has been looked upon as a form of 'cottage economy', corded and stuffed quilting belong to a very different tradition, with a decorative rather than a practical emphasis. Examples have been found in India, Iran and Turkey, and both techniques proved extremely popular in Europe, especially in the seventeenth and eighteenth centuries. While tricky, these are techniques with especially impressive results.

The 'Tristan' quilt (detail), c.1360–1400
Quilted linen with cotton-wadded trapunto work, 320 x 287 cm (126 x 113 in.)
V&A: 1391–1904

CORD QUILTING

Cord, or corded, quilting was worked on two layers of material (usually linen) probably from the thirteenth century onwards; the technique was particularly popular in Italy, France and Spain in this period, and often used for bed covers. In England it was and often still is known as 'Italian quilting'. A design is stitched using parallel lines of backstitch or running stitch; a cord is then run through the channel formed by these quilting stitches, creating a tactile, raised area, around which other stitches can be worked. This technique and trapunto work (see pp.60-67) often find contemporary expression in fashion and other textile arts.

An international technique

Examples of sixteenth-century corded work have been discovered in India, often incorporating hunting scenes with figures in European dress and combining cord quilting with other forms, including trapunto. The designs were destined for a European market. The technique of cord quilting reached a peak of popularity in Europe in the seventeenth and eighteenth centuries, when it was mainly used to decorate garments such as linen caps, women's jackets and petticoats, and men's waistcoats. Patterns of naturalistic flowers and leaves were corded and combined with other needlework techniques to create amazingly complex designs.

Cord quilting was worked in parts of northern and eastern Europe, including Germany, Poland, the Netherlands and Scandinavia and was taken up in North America later in the eighteenth century. The popularity of cord quilting does not appear to have continued into the nineteenth century, but the technique was revived in Europe during the 1920s and 1930s with the popularity of cord-quilted cushions and other furnishings.

Bed cover, 1720-50
Embroidered and cord-quilted linen,
251 x 236 cm (98⅞ x 92⅞ in.)
V&A: T.209-1983

Corset, c.1825–35

Cord quilting works to both decorative and functional effect
in this nineteenth-century corset. Concentrated down the
sides of the garment, in graphic, 'cross-hatched' patterns,
the quilting acts (in concert with the boning) to increase the
corset's rigidity and strength. Trapunto work (see pp.60–67)
also appears, on a busk around the diaphragm area, which
would work to flatten the stomach and lift the breasts of
the wearer. In contrast to this rigidity, soft gussets over the
breasts and hips allow for the natural curves of the body.

Cord-quilted cotton with silk trapunto work, waist: 51 cm (20⅛ in.)
V&A: T.57–1948

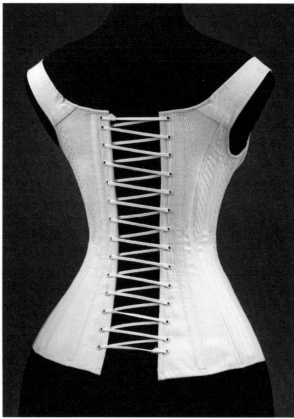

PINCUSHION

This small, graphic pincushion is monochrome, but the cord quilting – which can be achieved either by hand or using a sewing machine – creates a textured design that works especially well on silk fabric. The simple, linear pattern echoes the cording on the corset shown on the previous page and is a perfect introduction to the technique.

You will need

Handwoven or similar medium-weight silk (e.g. dupion) in a colour of your choice, one piece 18 x 18 cm (7 x 7 in.; for the front outer) and two pieces, each 17 x 11 cm (6³⁄₄ x 4¹⁄₄ in., for the back outer of the cushion)

Lightweight cotton, one piece 18 x 18 cm (7 x 7 in., for the front backing) and two pieces, each 17 x 11 cm (6³⁄₄ x 4¹⁄₄ in.; for the back of the cushion) **Note:** *The fabrics are much larger than the finished pincushion, which measures 9.5 x 9.5 cm/ 3¾ x 3¾ in., for ease of handling while machine sewing. If you are hand stitching instead, start with a smaller piece, approx. 13 x 13 cm/5¼ x 5¼ in.*

Tacking (basting) thread

General sewing thread, to match silk fabric

Knitting yarn, DK or Aran weight (ideally a loosely spun yarn)

Hand-sewing needle (or sewing machine)

Tapestry needle (blunt-pointed), with an eye large enough to accommodate two strands of yarn

Water-erasable marker

Toy stuffing

Pins

Embroidery, or other sharp, fine-pointed scissors

Project by Ruth Singer

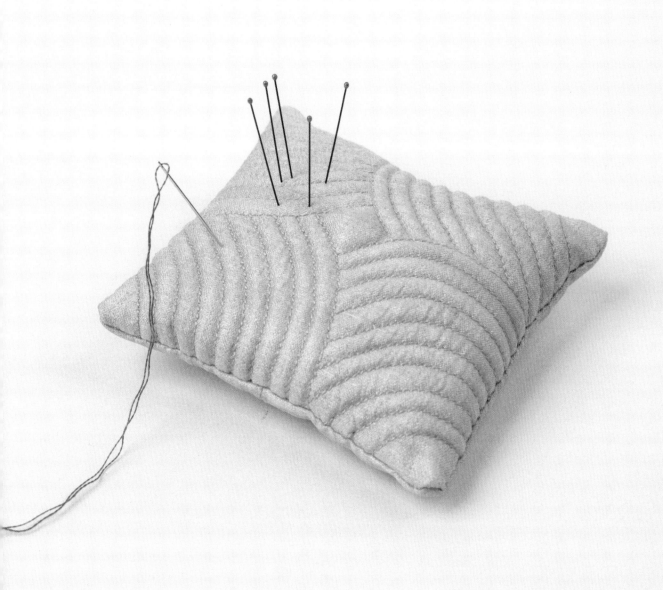

How to make

1 Trace the design template opposite onto the right side of the larger piece of silk fabric using water-erasable marker, positioning the design centrally (see p.16 for full instructions). Place the corresponding piece of cotton backing fabric beneath it and tack (baste) the two pieces of fabric together around the edges.

2 Start sewing the quilted channels about 2 cm (¾ in.) from the edge of the design and work inwards. Do not secure the ends of your thread; instead, leave threads long and, at the end, thread them to the back of the work, trim and knot. Stitch along the lines using a careful **running** or **backstitch** (see p.17) if sewing by hand, and a straight stitch if using a sewing machine, ensuring the lines don't overlap.

3 If necessary, remove any visible pen marks (see p.11). Dry and press.

4 Now you are ready to begin cording! You will need to test how many strands of yarn are required; try two strands to start with and adjust if the padding is too tight or too loose. Start with a 50-60 cm (20-24 in.) length. Thread the yarn into your tapestry needle, doubling it over and leaving the ends unknotted. Start with one of the shallower curves at the corners of the design. Feeding the needle between the layers of fabric, pull the cord almost all the way through, leaving approx. 2 cm (¾ in.) tails of yarn at each end. Cut and repeat for all the curves that are open-ended.

5 For the innermost curves, you will need to create a small hole in the backing fabric to bring the needle out at the end of the row. Try using the tapestry needle to do this, or, if this is too difficult, use your embroidery scissors to tease the weave apart, making sure you do not cut the stitching or silk material. Leave an approx. 1 cm (⅜ in.) tail on the yarn.

6 Give the whole piece a few tugs and smooth out the front to make sure no cords are pulled too tight and puckering the design. Cut a tiny hole in the backing of the central diamond and stuff lightly.

Feed the yarn through the stitched channels, starting in the corners, as instructed in steps 4 and 5.

7 Now prepare the back of the cushion, working with the silk fabric pieces and the corresponding cotton backing pieces. Place a cotton backing piece against the wrong side of each silk piece, and now treat each pair as one piece. Place the silk/cotton pairs silk sides together, matching up all the raw edges. Pin and sew along one long edge using a 1.5 cm (⅝ in.) seam allowance, leaving a 5 cm (2 in.) gap in the centre. Press the seam allowance open.

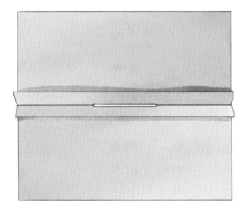

8 Now place the finished, corded front piece and the cushion back right sides together. Tack together around the edges. On the corded side, mark a 9.5 cm (3¾ in.) square around the design, and machine or hand sew around the entire square, neatly enclosing all the stitched ends of the design). Trim to a 1 cm (⅜ in.) seam allowance, cutting away any excess yarn.

9 Trim the seam allowance at the corners on the diagonal, then turn the whole right side out through the gap in the cushion back. Stuff as required, and then use **whip stitch** (see p.17) to close the gap and secure the rest of the back seam.

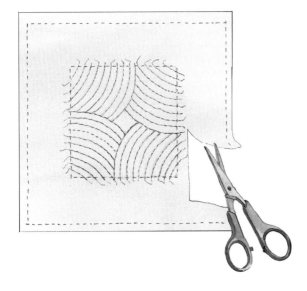

Now try...

A quilt block or cushion. This design could be adapted to create either; it is quite firm so, for a quilt, you may wish to alternate corded and uncorded rows. You could also try using a light, semi-transparent top fabric such as cotton lawn and coloured wool yarns to create a subtle rainbow effect.

Design template

Template shown at 100%

TRAPUNTO

Trapunto, or stuffed quilting (from the Italian *trapuntare*, to quilt), was known in Sicily as early as the thirteenth century. It is often confused with similar techniques used in making traditional wholecloth Provençal quilts (or *boutis*) from the seventeenth century onwards. Like cord quilting, the technique is worked on at least two layers of material, with outline patterns stitched using backstitch or running stitch. The design elements are then stuffed using a filling inserted through incisions or threads pulled apart in the backing (it is typically worked on an open-weave fabric), to create an area of high relief.

Then and now
One of the earliest surviving examples of this technique is the c.1360-1400 'Tristan' quilt, a Sicilian linen textile depicting scenes from the medieval legend of Tristan and Isolde (overleaf). The clear, pronounced effect of the trapunto must have looked particularly impressive by candlelight, with lively scenes of battles, ships and castles. Meanwhile, stuffed quilting is increasingly popular with contemporary quilters, who utilize its potential to embellish everything from traditional designs to freeform, impressionistic landscape quilts, and even with couturiers. The jackets in Schiaparelli's Autumn/ Winter 2016 couture collection are a case in point (see p.9) and nod to the use of trapunto in early designs by Elsa Schiaparelli herself (see opposite).

Elsa Schiaparelli, evening dress, designed 1935
Wool crêpe and gold braid
V&A: T.36-1964

The 'Tristan' quilt, c.1360–1400

The story represented on this quilted linen coverlet is that
of the oppression of Cornwall by King Languis of Ireland and
his champion Morold, and the battle of Sir Tristan with the
latter on behalf of his uncle King Mark – a medieval European
legend. Fourteen separate scenes have been executed, with
all of the figurative elements and lettering worked in brown
linen thread, while the backgrounds are worked in white
stitching (also linen thread), using backstitch throughout.
We know that the figures were probably stuffed while the
work was in progress, and the variation in the quality of
drawing and stitching indicates that the quilt was probably
a collaborative effort. We also know that the scenes have
been rearranged at some point in the object's history,
though the reason for this is unknown.

Quilted linen with cotton-wadded trapunto work,
320 x 287 cm (126 x 113 in.)
V&A: 1391–1904

LAMPSHADE WRAP

A lampshade wrap transforms a plain shade into a work of art, which changes again when the bulb is lit. The motif used for this project has been taken from the 'Tristan' quilt, shown on the previous page, and shows just how simple and enjoyable the trapunto technique can be. Make sure you use a low-energy bulb – conventional bulbs give off too much heat.

You will need

White, medium-weight linen fabric, lampshade height + 2 cm (¾ in.) x lampshade circumference + 10 cm (4 in.)
(The shade photographed here measures 15 x 52 cm/6 x 20½ in, so linen measuring 17 x 62 cm/6¾ x 24½ in. was used.)

Cotton muslin (gauze fabric) or similar, for lining, same dimensions as above

White/natural-coloured, straight-sided drum-style lampshade

Tacking (basting) thread

DMC Pearl Cotton, no.8: white (8)

General sewing thread, white

Hand-sewing needle

Water-erasable marker

Toy stuffing

Embroidery, or other sharp, fine-pointed scissors

Knitting needle, any size

Tweezers with fine, pointed tips

Clothes pegs/sewing clips

Fabric glue

Optional

13 cm (5 in.) embroidery hoop

Sewing machine, with associated threads

How to make

1 Trace the design template onto your lining fabric using the water-erasable marker, positioning the design centrally (see p.16). Repeat the design, placing motifs evenly, as your fabric dimensions allow, leaving at least 2 cm (¾ in.) between motifs and 5 cm (2 in.) at each end.

2 Place your linen fabric right side down and then place the lining fabric, marked side up, on top. Tack (baste) the two layers together around the edges and around the motifs.

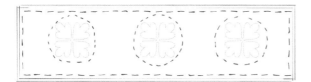

3 Work **running stitch** (see p.17) around the outline of each design using Pearl Cotton thread and stitches 1-2 mm (⅟₁₆ in.) long. Secure your thread in the lining fabric, and take care to keep the stitches even on the linen (front) side. **Tip:** *An embroidery hoop may help you to keep the fabric smooth.* When the stitching is complete, remove any visible pen marks if necessary (see p.11). Leave to dry, then remove the tacking and press.

4 Hem three of the edges before stuffing. Turn 1 cm (⅜ in.) to the lining side along both long edges and press. Machine or hand sew in place, stitching approx. 6 mm (¼ in.) from the folded edges. On one short edge only, make neat corners and then turn 1 cm (⅜ in.) to the lining side, and then press and stitch as before. Press again before stuffing. The other end is left unhemmed.

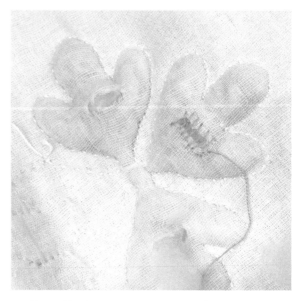

Stuff motifs from the reverse, as instructed in steps 5-7.

5 Each motif is padded using stuffing inserted through gaps in the lining fabric. You may be able to tease the threads apart with a needle to create a small hole. Alternatively, separate the front and lining layers by pinching the fabrics between your finger and thumb and carefully make a tiny snip in the lining fabric only, in the centre of a motif area.

6 Fluff up the stuffing and tease it into small, airy pieces, not rolled into balls or lumps. Use a knitting needle or other tool to gently push small amounts at a time into the motif. Fill around the edges of the shape first before filling the centre. Take care not to overfill. If the fabric puckers when you lay the piece flat then remove the stuffing, fluff it up and start again, working more gently. Use tweezers to remove or rearrange the stuffing.

7 Use general sewing thread to sew up the stuffing holes, but be careful not to pull too tight. When complete, press and steam the whole piece carefully around the motifs to remove creases. Do not press over the design – you will flatten it!

8 To make up the lampshade, first test the fit. Use pegs or sewing clips to hold the edges in place as you wrap the fabric around the lampshade. Trim the unhemmed edge if required so that there is only 2 cm (¾ in.) overlap. Remove the fabric, then apply a line of fabric glue along the lampshade's vertical seam. Stick the unhemmed end of the fabric to the glue, making sure it is straight and even. Check by wrapping the fabric around the lampshade again and then leave the glue to dry, holding the wrap in place with pegs or clips. To finish, apply glue on top of the unhemmed edge and bring the hemmed edge around to overlap. Hold in place with pegs or clips until dry.

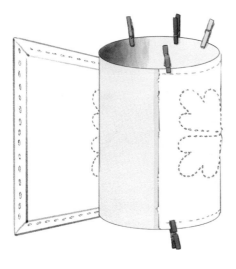

Now try...

Using a denser pattern repeat or varying the size of the motif. Covering more of the fabric in this way will allow less light through the finished wrap and create a lacy pattern. Alternatively, try a fine, semi-transparent fabric such as cotton lawn for the outer part of the wrap and coloured merino wool for the stuffing; the colours will show through the fabric and give a subtle coloured effect.

Design template

Template shown at 100%

GEOMETRIC

As a general rule, patchwork is made by joining small pieces of fabric together to create a patterned cloth (the linking of 'patchwork' and 'quilt' has come to be accepted, but, strictly speaking, much patchwork is unquilted and quilting has its own tradition). Surviving examples dating from between AD 700 and AD 800 – discovered in the 1920s in the Caves of the Thousand Buddhas, China – include a votive hanging made from patched triangles and rectangles; these reveal that the construction of true patchwork has changed little over hundreds of years. Geometric designs – using simple, uniform shapes in repeated arrangements, as opposed to the more freeform techniques – are found, historically, across Europe, Asia and the Americas. They evidence a shared concern with the preservation of precious fabrics and their designs speak to the sharing of influences through developing trade routes.

Bed cover, 1800–50
Pieced silk, 231 x 208 cm (91 x 81⅞ in.)
V&A: T.75–1937

PATCHWORK

BLOCK PATCHWORK

Relatively simple patchworks made up of repeating
blocks, like the quilts shown opposite and overleaf,
evidence arguably the most straightforward form
of patchworking, in which small, repeated units are
joined together in a regular, geometric pattern.
From the textiles and dyes used in historical quilts
of this kind, we have a way of dating them and
discovering something of their creators' origins.
The nineteenth-century, American tradition of block
quilts (with their increasingly complex 'block'
designs) is a prime example of this, with the quilts
forming a partial visual record of women's lives
in North America.

Pioneer quilts

North American pioneer women and their descendants
kept history and traditions alive and preserved in
the quilt blocks that were designed, sewn and passed
on to friends and family. These block patterns
might be inspired by historical events – 'Burgoyne
Surrendered' commemorates the battle of Saratoga
in 1777; by literature – the tales of Sir Walter
Scott are honoured in 'The Lady of the Lake'; or
by day-to-day events. They were valuable, with
collections of blocks or block albums even
mentioned in wills, and of great significance
in binding communities together.

Bed cover, early 18th century
Pieced, embroidered and appliquéd
silk, 190.5 x 135.5 cm (75 x 53⅜ in.)
V&A: 1475-1902

Bed cover, 1810–45

Accurate dating of objects such as this is difficult, as the textiles used (including printed panels, such as the one at the centre) were often stored for years before being added to the patchwork. In addition, a great range of fabrics has been used: from men's shirting cottons to a woollen blanket (which has been used for wadding), and even a 'printer's end' – the maker's mark, usually discarded, at the end of a length of printed cotton. While these fabrics can be used to date the quilt, broadly, to the early nineteenth century, it is only the central printed panel, which also appears in 'The Garden Coverlet' in the Rachel Kay-Shuttleworth Collection, Gawthorpe Hall, that secures the date between 1810 and 1845.

Pieced and quilted cotton, 268 x 270 cm (105½ x 106¼ in.)
V&A: T.17–1924

PICNIC QUILT

Using just one simple shape – the square – you can still create a bold and impressive quilt. Cut your fabrics carefully and neatly – after that, it's just a matter of assembly! Use either metric or imperial measurements throughout. Do not mix them, as the sizes are slightly different and your pieces will not fit together. Using a sewing machine to assemble and quilt makes this a relatively quick and achievable project.

You will need

Quilting cottons: 20 cm (¼ yd) each of chocolate brown, orange and taupe; 40 cm (½ yd) of teal; 60 cm (¾ yd) fuchsia (**Note:** *This project assumes all lengths are cut to width of fabric, WOF – approx. 107 cm, 42 in., wide as a minimum.*)

Binding fabric: 30 cm (⅜ yd), colour your choice

Backing fabric (ideally quilting cotton): 112 x 112 cm (44 x 44 in.)

Wadding (batting), 112 x 112 cm (44 x 44 in.)

General sewing thread, neutral or to match fabrics

Tacking (basting) thread or safety pins

Quilting thread, in a contrasting colour (see p.15)

Hand-sewing needle

Rotary cutter

Quilting ruler

Cutting mat

Pins

Sewing machine

Tailor's chalk or other erasable fabric marker

Optional

Walking (even-feed) sewing machine foot

Project by Jenny Haynes. Finished dimensions: 100 x 100 cm (40 x 40 in.)

How to make

1 Prepare all your fabric pieces. From each of the chocolate brown, orange and taupe fabrics, cut two 10 cm (4 in.) x WOF strips. Cut each strip into ten 10 x 10 cm (4 x 4 in.) squares, making a total of twenty squares of each colour (three of the taupe will not be used). From the teal fabric, cut four 10 cm (4 in.) x WOF strips. Cut into forty 10 x 10 cm (4 x 4 in.) squares (four will not be used). From the fuchsia fabric, cut six 10 cm (4 in.) x WOF strips. Cut into sixty 10 x 10 cm (4 x 4 in.) squares (eight will not be used).

2 Prepare your binding. From your binding fabric, cut five 5.5 cm (2¼ in.) x WOF strips.

3 You can now begin assembling blocks. Using a 6 mm (¼ in.) seam allowance throughout, join squares of fabric to form three-square strips, as shown in the illustration below. (You need to make thirty-nine strips in total; refer to the diagrams opposite for the fabric placement.) To make a strip, join the first two squares by placing them right sides together and hand- or machine-sewing along one edge (see p.16 for tips). Join a third square to the other side of your central square in the same way and press all seams open. **Note:** *Going forward, press all seams open after each step.*

Your finished quilt, showing all fabric placement

4 Using the strips you have just made, assemble thirteen nine-patch-squares (a nine-patch-square is simple one made up of nine squares), as shown in the illustration below.

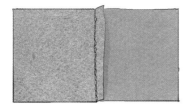 

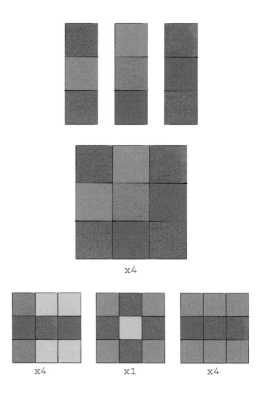

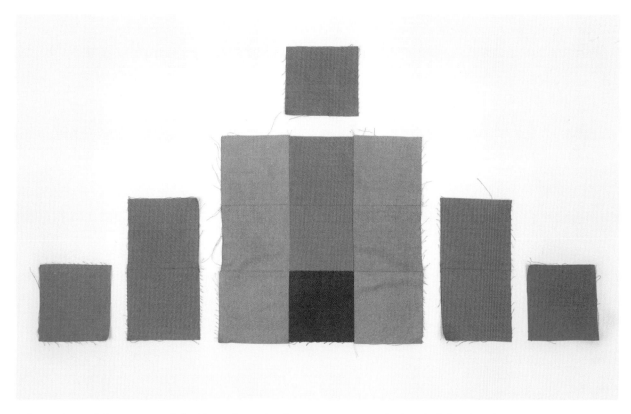

Join a nine-patch-square and further pieces to form a corner, as instructed in step 6.

5 Join nine-patch-squares as shown in the illustration below to create the central square of the quilt top.

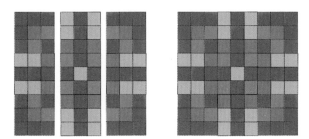

6 Following the photograph above, join the remaining nine-patch blocks and squares to form the four corner pieces of the quilt top. Remember to assemble linear strips in the first instance and then join these together to make each complete shape.

7 Following the illustration below, join each corner piece to the central square, aligning the long edge of each corner piece with an outer edge of the square.

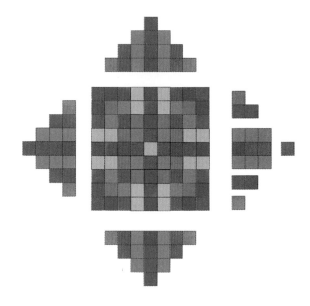

Square off the edges of your layered quilt (see step 11).

8 You can now assemble your quilt (leaving the 'sawtooth' edges of the top layer as they are for now). Lay your backing fabric, right side down, on a flat surface. Lay the wadding on top and smooth out any wrinkles. Lay the pieced top layer, right side up, over both layers and smooth again.

9 Pin or tack (baste) all three layers together, to avoid movement while the layers are quilted. For details about tacking, see p.47, step 8.

10 Quilt your layers together, sewing lines parallel to the seam lines or making a crosshatch pattern. If you have one, use a walking (even-feed) foot on your sewing machine, as this will prevent the top layer from being 'pushed' ahead as you stitch, causing puckering. You can use an erasable marker to mark straight lines to follow.

11 Using your quilting ruler and tailor's chalk, mark a line around the edge of the quilt, squaring off all edges (see photograph above). You will align your binding with this line in step 14.

12 Make and attach your quilt binding. Start by joining your strips: line the end of one piece up with the next – at right angles, right sides together – and mark a diagonal line from the top-right corner of the bottom strip to the bottom-left corner of the top strip, as shown below. Sew along this line and trim off the corner 6 mm (¼ in.) beyond the stitched line. Open up the seam and press. Join all the binding pieces in this way.

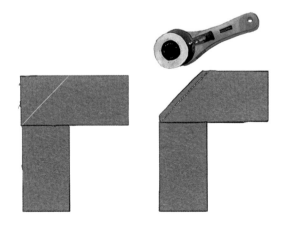

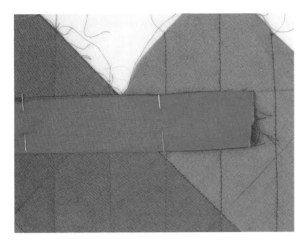

Pin the binding in place, along the chalk line.

13 Fold the entire binding strip in half lengthwise, wrong sides together, and press. Make sure ends are trimmed square.

14 With your quilt right side up, and starting part way along one edge, line up the double raw edge of your binding strip with your chalk line. Start pinning in place, 7.5 cm (3 in.) from the end of the binding strip. When you get to a corner, fold the binding strip away from the quilt at a 90-degree angle then double the strip back and start pinning along the next side. A peaked triangle will form in the corner. Continue to pin, stopping 7.5 cm (3 in.) before your first pin and leaving the binding overlapping in this space. Trim all layers flush to the outer edge of the pinned binding.

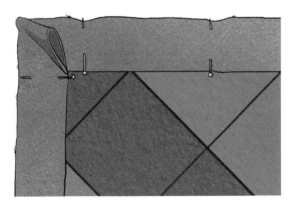

15 Starting at the first pin, sew the binding and quilt together along the straight edges, stopping and starting 6 mm (¼ in.) before and after each corner, and leaving the 7.5 cm (3 in.) overlap unsewn.

16 Lay the 7.5 cm 'tails' along the gap's edge. Fold back the extra length of both ends where they meet and press flat. Unfold the binding strips in this gap, line them up, right sides together and sew along the crease. Trim the seam allowance and press open. Refold the binding and sew to the quilt top, as above.

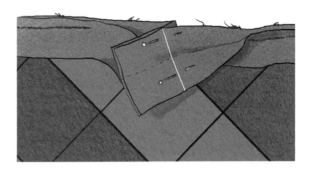

17 Fold the binding over to the back of the quilt. The binding's folded edge should just cover the stitching line where the binding was sewn to the front of the quilt. Pin in place around the whole quilt. When you reach the corners, finger press the binding so that it turns the corner at a 45-degree angle.

18 Using a hand-sewing needle and quilting thread, **slip stitch** (see p.17) the binding to the wrong side of the quilt.

Now try...

Your own design. Once you've got the hang of assembling blocks into a larger pattern, you can start to design your own quilt tops, using just squared paper and some colouring pencils! For a more elaborate quilt, you can combine these basic principles of assembly with some of the other block ideas in this book (see, for example, pp.84–91) to create your own unique quilt.

ENGLISH PAPER PIECING

A popular and accessible form of patchworking, English paper piecing – sometimes known as 'foundation piecing' or 'English patchwork' – gained in popularity in eighteenth-century England, where restrictions on the importing of Indian chintz meant that such fabrics were regarded as very precious. Every scrap of fabric mattered, and so remnants would be pieced together to form larger cloths, required for bed covers and curtains. The basic technique involves basting fabric pieces over paper templates (the hexagon is commonly associated with this method); these pieces are then sewn together using whip stitch and the paper templates usually removed. The resulting, often very intricate patterns, in combination with a variety of fabrics and colours, can generate kaleidoscopic effects. Compare this to North American block patchwork traditions, such as Amish patchwork (pp.92-97), where seaming is the more common method of construction.

Patchwork mosaics

The small, intricate, tessellating patterns of many English-paper-pieced items – constructed from fabrics pieced together in the shape of hexagons, crosses, octagons and diamonds, etc. – give them the alternative name 'mosaic' patchworks. Many such patchworks have survived with their original paper templates still intact and these – cut from old letters, bills and newspapers – can provide documentary evidence of the approximate date of an item's construction, as well as giving us a snapshot of the life and times of its maker.

Bed cover, 1860-70
Pieced silk, 79.5 x 40.2 cm
(31¼ x 15⅞ in.)
V&A: T.427-1980

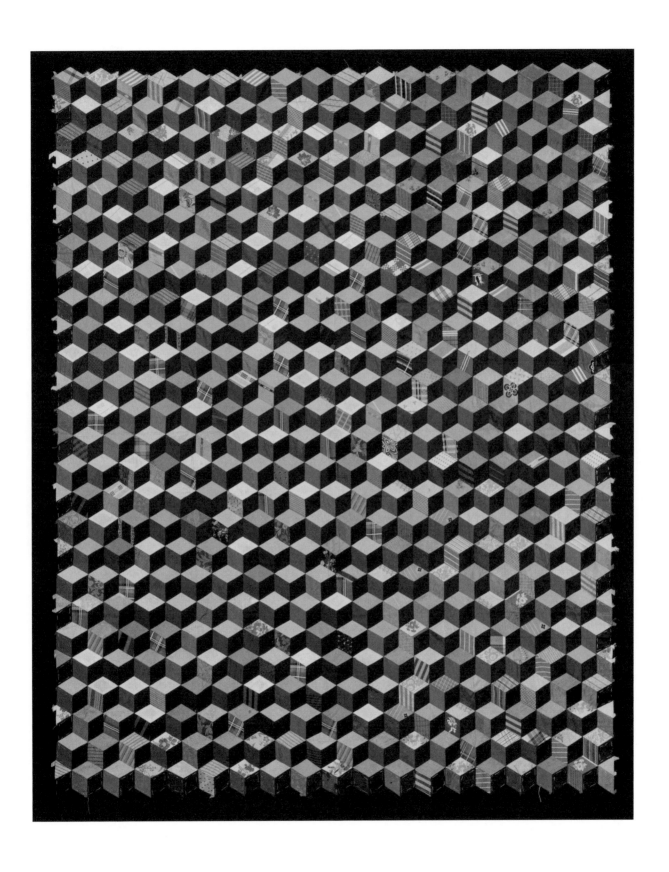

'Sundial' Coverlet, 1797

This 'coverlet' – referred to as such because it is pieced but not wadded – has been made from a wide range of contemporary block-printed cottons, the small-scale prints of which are typical of gowns of the period. While it incorporates some embroidery, the predominant technique on display is paper piecing and the combination of geometric and figurative designs, all worked over paper, evidences the considerable skill of its maker. She has created a microcosm of her world in cloth: surrounding the central timepiece are domestic tools such as a pincushion, needle and scissors; as the coverlet extends outwards, the subject matter also expands, first out into the garden and then out to the four pieced world maps in the corners. The range of textiles in the patchwork itself has been taken as evidence that the maker was in some way connected to the textile trade.

Pieced cotton, 302.3 x 279.4 cm (119 x 110 in.)
V&A: T.102–1938

THREE ENGLISH PAPER-PIECED BLOCKS

These English paper-pieced blocks are based on designs found in the patchwork coverlet shown on the previous page. The Liberty prints suggested here, as well as being bright and bold, are intended to reference the dress fabrics of the eighteenth-century original. You can cut your pieces at random or 'fussy cut', to ensure that motifs from your pattern are featured prominently in the finished blocks. Use either metric or imperial measurements throughout. Do not mix them, as the sizes are slightly different and your pieces will not fit together. Paper piecing is intricate work. Take your time and enjoy the process – the results are well worth it.

You will need

Quilting cotton (for piecing): fat quarters, fifteen different prints (block one); fat quarters, seven different prints (block two); fat quarters, three different prints (block three)

Quilting cotton (for three background squares): each 16.5 x 16.5 cm (6½ x 6½ in.)

Tacking (basting) thread

General sewing threads, in colours to match piecing fabrics

Hand-sewing needle

Tracing paper

Ruler

Pen or pencil

Scissors suitable for paper

Clear template plastic (if you wish to fussy-cut fabric designs; see p.15)

Embroidery or other sharp, fine-pointed scissors

Pins

Optional

Temporary-hold fabric glue

Project by Florence Knapp

How to make

Block One

This block is set 'on point', i.e., it is pieced and then rotated 45 degrees and appliquéd to a base fabric. The design is symmetrical, in imitation of the original, carefully planned coverlet (pp.82-83), though you can of course vary your own fabric choice and arrangement.

1 Use the template supplied opposite to trace off and cut out your paper pieces. You will need a separate paper piece for each part of the block, so trace and cut out one 'A' piece, four 'B' pieces and fifty-two 'C' pieces. **Tip:** *Each 'C' piece measures just 1.3 cm (½ in.) square – if you find this too fiddly, there's no reason why you can't enlarge the design on a photocopier and make a larger block!*

2 Use these paper templates to cut your fabric pieces, using the template and photos as a guide to fabric/colour choices. **Note:** *The paper templates do not include a seam allowance, which needs to be added. Fabric should be cut 6 mm (¼ in.) bigger all round than the paper templates. See p.16 for tips on cutting out.*

3 Tack (baste) each fabric piece to its respective paper template. Begin by placing the paper template centrally against the wrong side of the fabric piece. Fold over one seam allowance at a time and tack through the fabric and the paper using large stitches, which can be removed easily after piecing all the shapes together. **Tip:** *Specialist fabric glue can be used instead to temporarily attach the fabric to papers.*

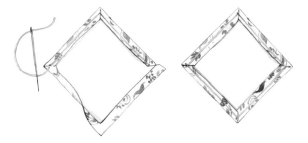

4 Lay out the individual pieces as you intend them to appear in the finished block. Begin assembly starting with the diagonal row of pieces that runs through the centre. Join together the two outer pairs of 'C' squares, and then join these with two 'B' pieces and the central 'A' to produce a strip like that shown below.

To sew, place two pieces face to face, carefully aligning the edges to be joined, and sew together using a hand-sewing needle and **whip stitch** (see p.17), catching just the folds of the fabric with your needle.

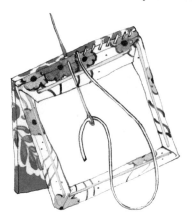

5 Sew the remaining pieces into diagonal rows in the same way. Finally, join the rows together, taking care to match up the seams to produce a neat finish.

6 Press and remove the papers, cutting the tacking stitches or teasing back the glued seams. Take care not to distort the smooth outer edge.

7 Once complete, appliqué the piecing to the 16.5 x 16.5 cm (6½ x 6½ in.) background square, using **slip stitch** (see p.17), making sure it is placed centrally. For this task, use a thread colour that blends well with the piecing, rather than the background fabric.

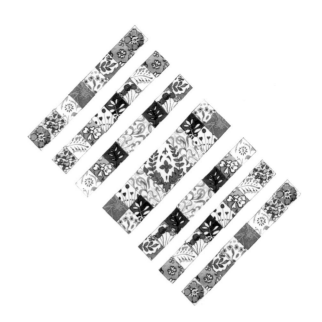

Template

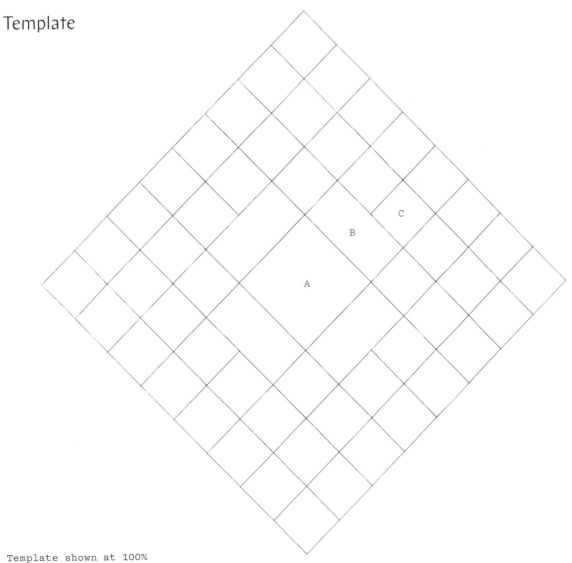

Template shown at 100%

Block Two

One of the key features of this block in the quilt shown on pp.82-83 is the thoughtful placement of fabrics in the round of diamonds, which we've tried to replicate; you can see that the four fabrics used here are arranged symmetrically around the vertical axis.

1 See steps 1-3 on p.86 for instructions on how to prepare your fabric; using the template opposite, cut one 'A' piece and twelve each of the 'B', 'C' and 'D' pieces, remembering to add seam allowances.
Tip: *Be mindful to tack the outer curve of the 'D' pieces with a firm, confident hand to produce a smooth edge, using a few more tacking stitches or a little extra temporary fabric glue if needed.*

2 Start by joining pieces 'B', 'C' and 'D' as per the illustration below (see also step 4 on p.86). Create this trio of pieces twelve times over.

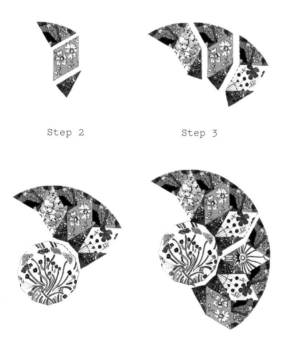

Step 2   Step 3

Step 4   Step 5

3 Lay out these little sets of shapes in the order in which you'd like them to appear. Take the first three and sew them together as shown left. Continue to work in this way to produce four sets of shapes.

4 If you have used a directional print for the central piece, 'A', be mindful of which way up it goes and sew on the first set of shapes as shown left.

5 Sew on the next set of shapes. To avoid the seams coming out of alignment over the course of a long seam, it's best to sew in shorter stretches; start at the point denoted by a dot in the illustration and sew out to each side in turn. **Tip:** *It is perfectly normal to have to gently fold your work in order to align some edges.*

6 See steps 6-7 on p.87 for instructions on how to finish the piecing and appliqué the finished motif to the background square.

Template

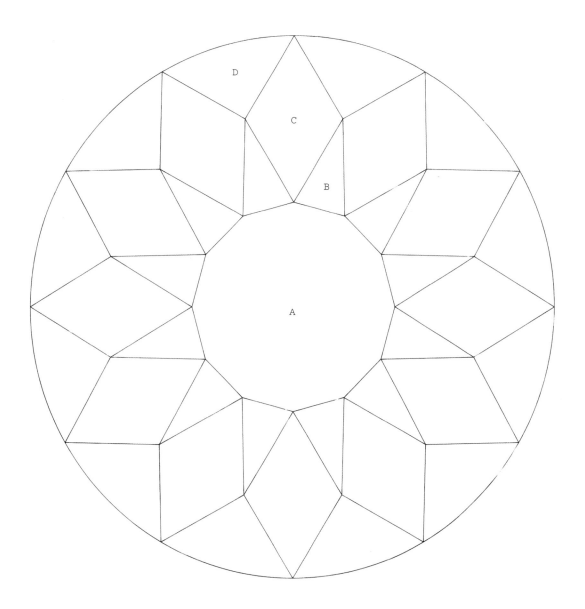

Template shown at 100%

Block Three

There is only one shape to piece in this block, so the interest comes from the use of fabric and colour placement. We have arranged two prints alternately around the central hexagon, in imitation of the quilt shown on pp.82-83.

1   See steps 1-3 on p.86 for instructions on how to prepare your fabric; using the template opposite, cut a hexagon in one print for the central shape and three hexagons in each of the other two prints for the outer ring, remembering to add seam allowances.

2   Join the central hexagon to one of the outer hexagons as in the illustration below (see also step 4 on p.86).

3   Continue sewing in this way, joining each hexagon as shown in the illustration below. When sewing, only attempt to align two edges at a time and keep in mind that in order to get the pieces to align, you may need to temporarily fold your work.

A note on templates

You can create templates from clear plastic to speed up fabric cutting and allow you to carefully position and cut particular motifs from the fabric – if you choose to do so, remember to add on a seam allowance, so that the cut fabric pieces are also large enough to wrap around your papers.

Step 2   Step 3

Now try...

4   See steps 6-7 on p.87 for instructions on how to finish the piecing and appliqué the finished motif to the background square.

Using the blocks in bigger projects. These blocks can be framed once completed, or incorporated into other projects such as cushion covers or place mats. Used in repeat, they could be the starting point for an entire quilt top (see p.74).

Template

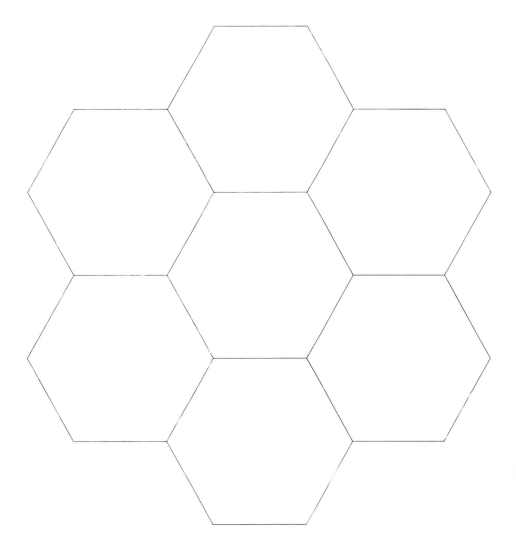

Template shown at 100%

AMISH PATCHWORK

North Americans set great store by their traditions of patchwork, which grew out of the varied cultures of their immigrants. Amish communities came to North America from Alsace, Switzerland and southern Germany between 1727 and 1850, and settled mainly in Pennsylvania, Ohio and Indiana. Their famous quilts are made of plain, lightweight woollen cloth or cotton fabrics in strong colours – scarlet, burgundy, emerald, coral, purple, navy blue, black and turquoise – and are often characterized by bold, simple pieced designs with elaborate, all-over quilting. They are part of a plain, yet elegant design aesthetic, seen also in Amish furniture and building.

A booming craft

Today, Amish quilts are considered highly desirable by many outside the strictly religious communities in which they originate. In Lancaster County, Pennsylvania – home to a large Amish community – many women have opened small shops to sell their creations. Not only this, but large-scale quilting events take place several times a year, with classes, seminars and displays forming a large-scale version of the 'quilting bees' that are an important social occasion for Amish women. Traditionally, quilts were made as part of a dowry, or to be presented as gifts.

'Bar'-pattern quilt, c.1890s
Private collection

'Diamond in a Square' quilt, 1820–30

Lancaster County in Pennsylvania is the site of the oldest continuously occupied Amish community in the United States, and its quilts are distinct from those found elsewhere. This particular woollen quilt, with its square shape and wide borders and binding, is typical of the region, and its design – the 'diamond in a square' pattern, considered outdated by the wider quilting community in the early twentieth century – is virtually unique to the area. Note the scrolling feather-pattern quilting, the placement of which echoes the colourful piecing 'on top'. Generally, the less embellishment, the older an Amish quilt can be assumed to be.

Pieced, quilted wool, 193 x 193 cm (76 x 76 in.)
The American Museum in Britain: 1997.102

DIAMOND-IN-A-SQUARE QUILT

This quilt – its simple geometric design based on the example shown on the previous page – is surprisingly quick to piece, so it's easy to try different colour combinations before proceeding to hand-quilt your favourite version. In traditional Amish quilts, only plain, non-printed fabrics in a limited range of colours are used, but you could experiment with prints and palettes to achieve a different feel. Just make sure your fabric cutting is accurate! Use either metric or imperial measurements throughout. Do not mix them, as the sizes are slightly different and your pieces will not fit together.

You will need

Quilting cottons: 30 cm (⅓ yd) of fabric A (dark blue, for central on-point square); 20 cm (¼ yd) of fabric B (pale blue/grey, for central square triangles and outer border corners); 10 cm (⅛ yd) of fabric C (pale pink, for inner border strips); one fat eighth of fabric D (red, for inner border corners); 25 cm (⅜ yd) of fabric E (purple, for outer border strips)
Dressweight cotton or calico, for backing, 74 x 74 cm (29 x 29 in.)
Fabric for binding, colour your choice: 15 cm (¼ yd)
Wadding (batting), approx. 74 x 74 cm (29 x 29 in.)
Neutral-coloured general sewing thread
Quilting thread
Tacking (basting) thread or safety pins
Hand-sewing needle or sewing machine
Cutting mat
Rotary cutter
Quilting ruler
Pins
Erasable marker

Optional

Quilting hoop
Quilting needle
Thimble

Project by Pippa Moss. Finished dimensions: 63 x 63 cm (24¾ x 24¾ in.)

How to make

Note: *A 5 mm (¼ in.) seam allowance is used throughout.*

1   Cut one 26 x 26 cm (10 in.) square from fabric A for the central on-point square.

2   Cut two 20.5 x 20.5 cm (8 x 8 in.) squares from fabric B. Cut each once on the diagonal to give four triangles. **Note:** *Squares should be cut on the straight grain.* Line up the long edge of one triangle with one side of the central diamond, matching the centre points of each (it is best to press the pieces to find these centre points). Pin, right sides together, and hand- or machine-sew the seam using the neutral-coloured thread (see p.16 for tips). Repeat for the opposite triangle, and then the remaining pair. Press seams towards the triangles.

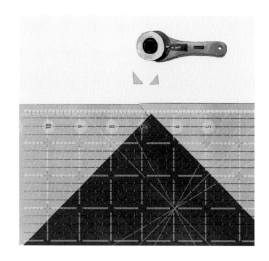

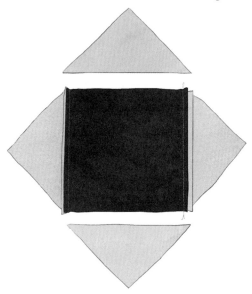

3   These triangles will need to be trimmed slightly. Working from the right side of your pressed piece, take your quilting ruler and align the 5 mm (¼ in.) marking with the corner of the central diamond. If your ruler has a 45° marking, align this with the side of your diamond. There should be a narrow sliver of cloth beyond your ruler, which can be cut off. Repeat for all four sides. The central square should now measure 36 x 36 cm (14 x 14 in.).

4   Add the inner border. Cut two 5 cm (2 in.) wide strips across the width of fabric C. Sub-cut to give four 5 x 36 cm (2 x 14 in.) strips. Right sides together and matching up the raw edges, join a strip to one side of the central square. Repeat on the opposite side. **Tip:** *When triangles are pieced, the stitches form an 'X'. Make sure that, when you sew on the borders, your seam line goes through this 'X' to give the diamond really sharp points.*

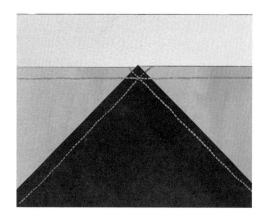

Join strips of fabric C and smaller squares of fabric D to form the inner border, as per step 5.

5 Cut four 5 x 5 cm (2 x 2 in.) squares from fabric D. Join one square to each end of the two remaining fabric C strips. Now sew these pieced strips to the remaining two sides of the central square.

6 Add the outer border. Cut two 11 cm (4½ in.) wide strips across the width of fabric E. Sub-cut to give four 11 x 44 cm (4½ x 17½ in.) strips. Right sides together and matching up the raw edges, join a strip to one side of the central square. Repeat on the opposite side.

7 Cut four 11 x 11 cm (4½ x 4½ in.) squares from fabric B. Join one square to each end of the two remaining fabric E strips. Now sew these pieced strips to the two remaining sides of your central square. Give the piece a final press (seams should all be pressed outwards) and remove any stray threads.

8 You are now ready to quilt! Photocopy or otherwise enlarge the templates opposite to full size. Photocopy the scrolled circle again at printed size, i.e. 50%. First position and transfer your quilting designs using an erasable marker (see p.16 for further instruction). Once the markings are in place, lay your backing fabric, right side down, on a flat surface and smooth out your wadding (batting) over the top. Lay the marked top, right side up, over both layers and smooth again. Pin or tack (baste) all three layers together: see p.47, step 8. **Note:** *Traditionally, the Amish hand-quilted their items, although you can use a machine if you prefer.*

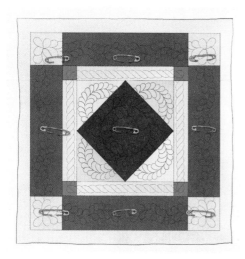

9 Using quilting thread in a dark colour, hand-quilt following the designs you have marked. Start in the centre of the quilt and work outwards (see p.48 for further instruction).

10 Bind and finish. Trim the excess backing and wadding (batting) level with the quilt top edges. Cut four 3 cm (1¼ in.) wide strips to the width of the binding fabric. Trim to make four 3 x 66.5 cm (1¼ x 26 in.) strips. Working from the right side, right sides together and matching up the raw edges, join a strip to the top and bottom of the quilt. Leave the same overhang at each end. Fold the binding over to the back of the quilt, turn under the long raw edges and then **slip stitch** in place (see p.17).

Apply binding to your finished quilt.

11 Trim the short ends of the binding flush with the side edges of the quilt top. In the same way, add the two remaining strips to each side of the quilt, but this time, before folding the binding over to the back of the quilt, turn under the short raw ends to neaten the corners. **Note:** *Amish quilts do not have mitred binding – it would be considered wasteful.*

Now try...

'Non-Amish' colours. Pastels, earth tones, yellow, orange and white would be equally effective in this design, as would prints or, for example, batik fabrics. The pattern can easily be enlarged to make a full-sized quilt.

Quilting templates

SEMINOLE PIECING

The characteristic structural patchwork of the Seminole people of Florida, North America – they are descended from indigenous peoples that for thousands of years have occupied the southeastern portion of North America, including this state – developed in the late nineteenth and early twentieth centuries, at a time when most other elements of this people's traditional culture had been lost. These patchwork fabrics were incorporated into clothing and never quilted. They were made by joining strips of cloth lengthwise into long, multi-coloured bands, cutting these bands into segments and assembling them in a pre-planned order into long bands of geometric pattern.

Cultural history

While the Seminoles were not inventors of the strip-piecing method, their patchwork does exemplify its aesthetic possibilities; their colourful clothing is the most visible art form of Seminole culture. Early documentation of Seminole patchwork designs takes the form of photographs from the Seminole exhibition villages in which many families took refuge from the 1920s onwards.

In 1821, Florida had officially come under the control of the United States; by 1858, after the three Seminole Wars, the nation had dwindled to just several hundred indigenous people. Government agents found these, now small, tribal groups in 1880 and established trading posts, where Seminole people gained access to cloth, needles, beads, food staples and metal tools. It was the introduction of the sewing machine (as well as the new fabrics and trimmings) that caught the creative imagination of Seminole women and transformed Seminole dress.

Skirt, 1950–70

The Ah-Tah-Thi-Ki Museum, on the Big Cypress Seminole
Indian Reservation in Florida, USA, houses more than 180,000
Seminole artefacts, including this long (106.7 cm/42⅛ in.)
patchwork skirt. A side panel of mismatched patchwork is likely
to have come from a later outfit, but the main, original part of
the skirt consists of seven orange bands, three bands of striped
print and three bands of patchwork; two of these patchwork
bands are of the 'cross' or 'sacred fire' pattern and the last is
a modified version of the design known as 'man on horse'.

Cotton, 106.7 x 161.3 cm (42⅛ x 63½ in.)
Ah-Tah-Thi-Ki Museum: 1996.55

STRIP-PIECED CUSHION

This cushion looks impressive, but is surprisingly easy to assemble once you've mastered a few basic techniques. The piecing should be done by machine as seams done by hand in running stitch are not secure enough to be cut and then re-joined. Make sure you keep all your cut pieces carefully organized to aid assembly. Use either metric or imperial measurements throughout. Do not mix them, as the sizes are slightly different and your pieces will not fit together.

You will need

Quilting cotton, 10 cm (⅛ yd) each of blue, red, cream and green; 20 cm (¼ yd) each of orange and yellow; 70 cm (¾ yd) black. (**Note:** *This project assumes all lengths are cut to width of fabric, WOF – approx. 107 cm or 42 in. wide as a minimum.*)

3 mm (⅛ in.) wide ribbon, 1.1 m (1¼ yd) each in three colours (we suggest black and two contrasting colours)

46 x 46 cm (18 x 18 in.) cushion pad (pillow form)

Machine-sewing threads, grey or neutral, black and to match your ribbons

Sewing machine

Rotary cutter

Cutting mat

Quilting ruler

Pins

Optional

Erasable marker or tailor's chalk

Black ric-rac, 1 m (1¼ yd)

Project by Jenny Barlow

How to make

1 Consult the chart on p.109 throughout, to help you keep your cut strips of fabric and finished rows organized.

2 Row 1. Cut one orange strip measuring WOF x 3 cm (1¼ in.) wide and one blue strip WOF x 2.5 cm (1 in.) wide. Place the strips right sides together and sew along one long edge, making a seam 5 mm (¼ in.) wide. **Note:** *You will use this seam allowance throughout.* Press open the pieced strip and press the seam towards the wider (orange) fabric.

3 Repeat step 2 with a 3 cm (1¼ in.) green and a 2.5 cm (1 in.) red strip, this time pressing the seam towards the narrow fabric.

4 Cut both pieced strips into 4 cm (1½ in.) wide segments.

5 Turn the segments of each pieced strip through 90 degrees and rejoin to form new strips, with the colours alternating, as shown below. Press seams in one direction.

6 Join the two new strips together along one long edge. Take care to match the seams. You've finished your first row!

7 Row 2. Cut one yellow strip WOF x 5 cm (2 in.) wide and a piece of ribbon or black ric-rac to the same length. Stitch the ribbon or ric-rac in place down the centre of the right side of the WOF strip, using thread that matches the ribbon or ric-rac. You might find it helpful to first fold the WOF in half widthwise and lightly finger press to give you a centre-line crease along which to align the ribbon or ric-rac.

8 Row 7. Cut one yellow strip WOF x 6.25 cm (2½ in.) wide and two pieces of ribbon, in contrasting colours, to the same length. Sew the ribbons to the right side of the fabric strip as described in step 7, making sure they are evenly spaced.

9 Row 3. Cut one red, one cream and one blue strip, each WOF x 3.5 cm (1½ in.) wide. Join the red to the cream strip, along the long edges. Join this strip to the blue in the same way, with the cream strip and blue abutting. Sew the second seam in the opposite direction to prevent 'bowing'. Press seams downwards.

10 Now cut the strip into 5 cm (2 in.) wide segments, at a 60-degree angle to the edge of the strip. The easiest way to do this is using a rotary cutter, cutting mat and the 60-degree line on a quilting ruler, as shown in the photograph opposite.

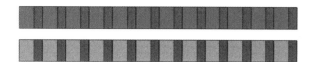

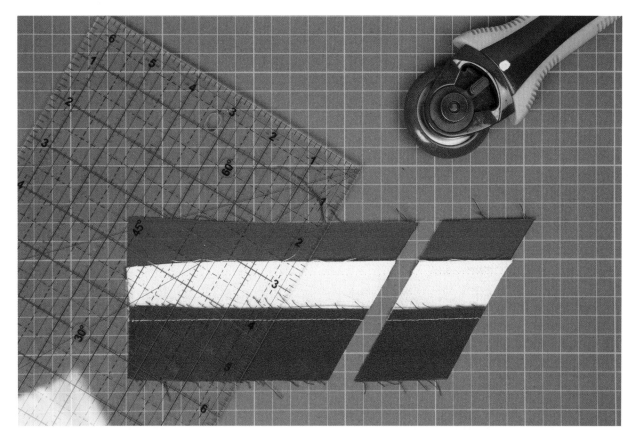

For row 3, cut your pieced strips into 5 cm (2 in.) segments, at a 60-degree angle, as instructed in step 10.

11 Rearrange the segments following the illustration below, making sure the seams of the cream sections match up, as shown. Pin and then sew the segments together. Press all the seams in the same direction.

12 Trim the long jagged edges as per the illustration below, making sure you leave at least 5 mm (¼ in.) beyond the top and bottom corners of the cream sections. It's easiest to do this using a rotary cutter, cutting mat and quilting ruler.
Tip: *It is very easy to stretch and distort the pieces in this row, so take care when handling.*

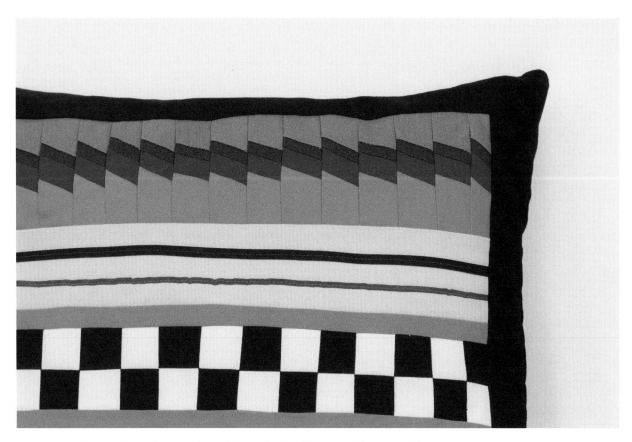

As you complete each strip, put it aside ready for final cushion assembly.

13 Rows 4 and 6. Cut two orange strips WOF x 2.5 cm (1 in.) wide.

14 Row 5. Cut one cream and one black strip, each WOF x 3.5 cm (1½ in.). Join these together along the long edges, as described in step 2, pressing the seam towards the black fabric.

15 Cut the pieced strip into 3.5 cm (1½ in.) wide segments. Rejoin the segments, rotating alternate segments to form a chequerboard pattern. Press all the seams in the same direction.

16 Row 8. Cut one orange and one green strip, each WOF x 5 cm (2 in.) wide. Cut one red strip WOF x 2.5 cm (1 in.) wide. Cut one blue strip WOF x 2 cm (¾ in.) wide.

17 Join all of these strips together on their long edges, starting with the orange and red, then attaching the blue and green in turn, as shown below. Sew adjacent seams in opposite directions to help prevent the pieced strip from 'bowing'. Press all the seams in the same direction.

18 Cut the strip into 3.5 cm (1½ in.) wide segments, at a 60-degree angle to the edge of the strip, as shown below. (**Note:** *The pieced strip is shown right side up.*) The easiest way to do this is using a rotary cutter, cutting mat and a quilting ruler.

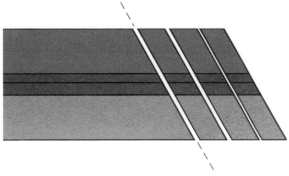

Cut at 60-degree angle

19 Rearrange the segments as per the illustration below, making sure the seams of the blue sections match up as shown, with the bottom seam of one blue section matching the top seam of the blue to its left. Pin and sew the segments together. Press all the seams in the same direction.

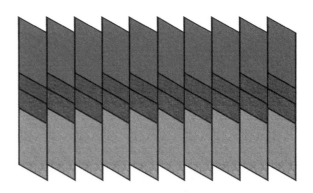

20 Trim the long jagged edges, as per the illustration below. The strip should measure approx. 9 cm (3½ in.) high – in our cushion, the bottom right-hand corners of the blue sections run along the centre of the strip.

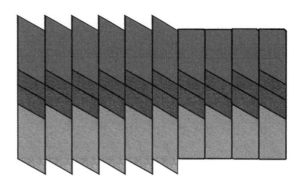

21 To complete the centre of the cushion top, sew the rows together, pressing after joining each strip. **Note:** *The rows will be different lengths, so align the ends of the rows at one side.*

22 Trim the panel so that all the edges are straight. We trimmed our panel to a square, but you could trim it to make a rectangle if you prefer.

23 From the black fabric, cut two 5.5 cm (2¼ in.) x WOF strips. Measure the height of the panel and from one WOF cut two strips of this measurement; join one strip to each side of the panel. Next, measure the width of the panel and cut two strips to this measurement; add one strip to the top and one to the bottom of the panel.

24 From the remaining black fabric, cut two cushion back pieces. These pieces should each match the dimensions of the cushion top, plus 5.5 cm (2¼ in.) in the width measurement. Our cushion top measured 46 x 46 cm (17½ x 17½ in.), so we cut two pieces, each 51.5 x 46 cm (19¾ x 17½ in.).

25 Take one of the back panels and fold a 1.5 cm (½ in.) hem to the wrong side along the shorter edge. Press. Fold this neatened short edge over to the wrong side again, this time by 18 cm (7 in.), and press. Using matching thread, topstitch near the fold of the hemmed edge to secure the folded layers together. Topstitch again, 1.5 cm (½ in.) below the folded edge. Repeat for the second cushion back rectangle.

26 Place the cushion top right side up on a flat surface and, matching up raw edges, place one cushion back piece on top, with the folded edge running across the cushion top as shown below. Then, in the same way, place the second cushion back piece over both of these - the two cushion back pieces will overlap. Pin or clip all around to secure all of the layers in position.

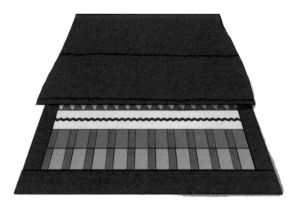

27 Sew all around the cushion with a 5 mm (¼ in.) seam. If you wish, sew a double line of stitching where the cushion back pieces overlap, for extra strength. Carefully clip the corners and, if desired, finish the seams with a zigzag stitch to neaten the raw edges. Turn right side out and press. Insert the cushion pad to finish. Using a slightly larger cushion pad will give you a nice plump cushion.

Now try...

Getting creative. Once you have mastered the technique, Seminole-inspired pieced fabric can be made into whatever you like. Try a notebook cover, a tote bag, edging for an apron or cuffs on a shirt. Add tabs to one end of a long rectangular panel for a curtain or hanging. Use the traditional bright colours, or choose more muted fabrics to match your home's colour scheme.

Chart

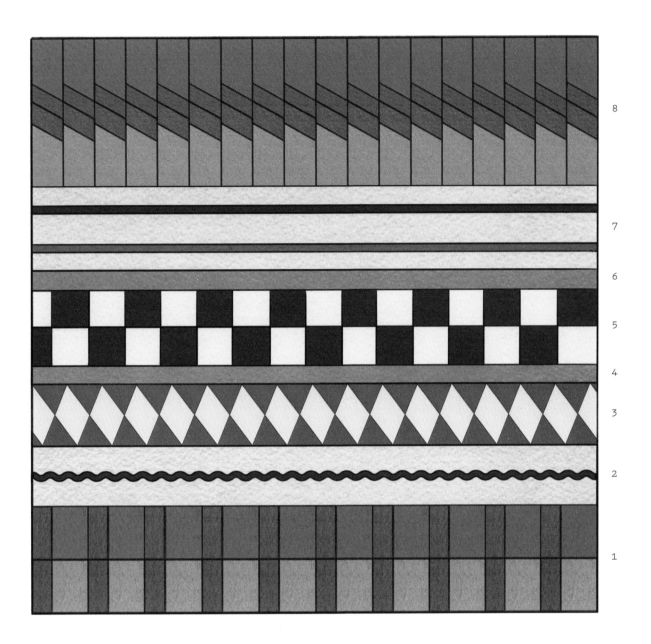

8

7

6

5

4

3

2

1

LOG CABIN

'Log cabin' quilts consist of an arrangement of blocks, each one formed of strips of light and dark fabrics that echo the timber structure of a traditional log cabin. These blocks are joined together in various orientations to create dramatic overall designs through their combinations of light and dark tonal values. Historically, the 'log cabin' pattern was one of the most popular in Western patchworking, especially in North America. It is possible to create quilt blocks to this design using cutting templates and following intricately planned designs, or the basic block can be constructed using a more improvisatory, 'strip-piecing' technique, whereby the maker starts with a central square of cloth and adds thin strips to the edges in sequence until a complete square is formed.

Dazzling geometry

Improvisatory strip patchwork reached an apogee in the quilts of Gee's Bend (officially, Boykin) – a small, remote, African-American community on the Alabama river, US. These unique, dazzling quilts, dating from the early 1920s to the present, are usually fundamentally geometrical – composed of strips, squares and other repeating geometrical units – but are often characterized by an idiosyncratic approach to colour, construction and the re-use of a range of recycled fabrics. Exciting patching results from bringing together existing designs such as 'log cabin' with approximately measured piecing.

Quilt ('Log Cabin, Barnraising Variation'), c.1865

The bold overall scheme of this quilt, made in Pennsylvania in the late nineteenth century, belies the extraordinary variety of fabric types and prints used in its construction. Each 'block' measures only 16 cm (6¼ in.) wide and yet comprises seventeen individual fabric strips: a range of solids and prints, dark and pale colour palettes. We cannot know how or if such a quilt was planned or improvised (you will note that fabric placement is not strictly symmetrical) but the result testifies to a maker with a keen eye for colour and tone, as well as a great deal of patience!

Pieced wool, silk and printed cotton, 223.5 x 223.5 cm (88 x 88 in.)
Los Angeles County Museum of Art: M.86.134.19

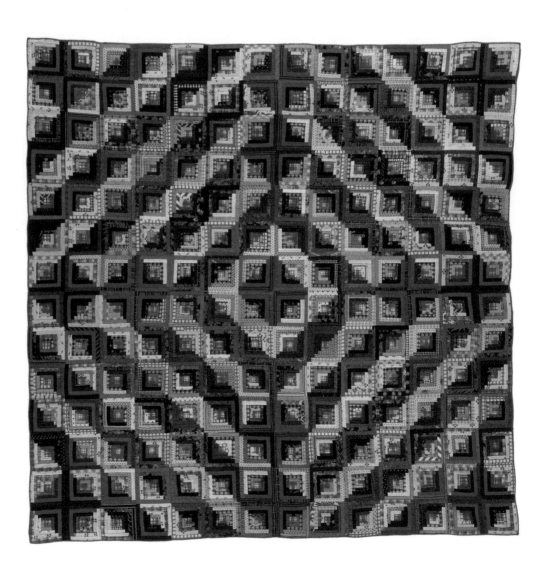

CURVED LOG-CABIN QUILT

Like many traditional quilts, those from Gee's Bend were often made from recycled work clothes and dresses, feed sacks and fabric remnants. You could follow this example; use shirts, scraps and fabric remnants, or even vintage bedding, cut into strips, to make the bold 'Log Cabin' quilt shown here. The key is to divide light and dark fabrics, so as to make the most of the design potential of the curved Log Cabin block. Use either metric or imperial measurements throughout. Do not mix them as the sizes are slightly different and your pieces will not fit together. This is a bed-sized quilt so will require time and patience, but the techniques involved are straightforward once you find your rhythm.

You will need

Quilting cottons, dark: 15 cm (¼ yd) each of fourteen different fabrics, each cut into three 5 cm (2 in.) x WOF strips; 10 cm (⅛ yd) of one fabric, cut into one 7.5 cm (3 in.) x WOF strip; 40 cm (½ yd) of one fabric, cut into eight 5 cm (2 in.) x WOF strips (for pieces 16a and 16b). (**Note:** *This project assumes all lengths cut to width of fabric, WOF – approx. 107 cm (42 in.) wide as a minimum – unless you are using remnants*)

Quilting cottons, light: 10 cm (⅛ yd) each of four different fabrics, each cut into one 7.5 cm (3 in.) x WOF strip; 20 cm (¼ yd) each of nine different fabrics, each cut into two 9 cm (3½ in.) x WOF strips; 20 cm (¼ yd) each of eight different fabrics, each cut into two 10 cm (4 in.) x WOF strips

Fabric for binding: a total of 70 cm (¾ yd) in a colour/s of your choice

Wadding (batting), 250 x 235 cm (99 x 92 in.)

Quilting cotton for backing, 4 m (4⅜ yd) if 107 cm (42 in.) wide or 2 m (2¼ yd) if double-width, i.e. 274 cm (108 in.)

Tacking (basting) thread

Neutral-coloured general sewing thread

Hand-quilting thread, e.g. DMC Pearl Cotton, no.8: selection of different contrasting colours

Embroidery/crewel needle, size 7

Sewing machine

Pins

Quilting ruler

Rotary cutter

Dressmaking scissors

Safety pins or quilters' safety pins

Optional

Tailor's chalk

Quilting hoop

Thimble

¼ in.-wide tape

Project by Jenny Haynes. Finished dimensions: 174 x 195 cm (68½ x 76¾ in.)

How to make

1 Cut your fabric strips as per the instructions on p.112, keeping them grouped by colour and width. In this quilt, darker fabrics were used for the concave, outer edge and lighter fabrics for the centre. The quilt is made of four blocks, two of block A and two of block B.

Block B   Block A

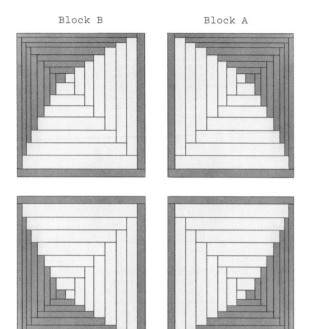

Block A   Block B

Assembly of Block A

2 Take one dark and one light 7.5 cm (3 in.) strip and cut a 7.5 cm (3 in.) piece from each. The dark square is piece 1 and the light square is piece 2a. Sew pieces 1 and 2a, right sides together, with a 5 mm (¼ in.) seam allowance. Press seams open.

3 Sew the new piece to the long edge of a 9 cm (3½ in.) light strip (piece 2b), right sides together, with a 5 mm (¼ in.) seam allowance. Press seams open. After sewing and pressing, trim the long strip flush using a rotary cutter (or scissors) and a ruler (see above right).

4 Continue to add pieces in the same way, by joining strips, pressing and then trimming (putting aside remnants for re-use). Note that you will be adding pieces in an anti-clockwise direction. Refer to the list opposite, and the illustrations below and opposite, following the sequence carefully. Note that pieces 16a and 16b are dark.

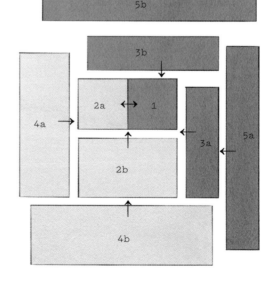

Piece strips in order, trimming the pieces level with the edges of the block before adding more strips, as instructed in step 3.

The widths of the strips are as follows:

Light
2a: 7.5 cm (3 in.)
2b: 9 cm (3½ in.)
4a: 7.5 cm (3 in.)
4b: 9 cm (3½ in.)
6a: 7.5 cm (3 in.)
6b: 9 cm (3½ in.)
8a: 9 cm (3½ in.)
8b: 10 cm (4 in.)
10a: 9 cm (3½ in.)
10b: 10 cm (4 in.)
12a: 9 cm (3½ in.)
12b: 10 cm (4 in.)
14a: 9 cm (3½ in.)
14b: 10 cm (4 in.)

Dark
1 : 7.5 cm (3 in.)
All other strips: 5 cm (2 in.)

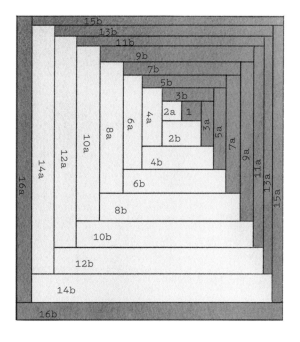

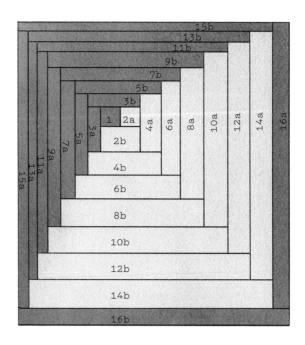

5 Your block A, should look like the photograph above. Add the final two outer pieces (16a and 16b), then make a second block in exactly the same way.

Assembly of Block B

6 Block B is made in the same way as block A (see steps 1-4), but the block is a mirror-image. So, this time, sew piece 2a to the right-hand edge of piece 1 and then add pieces in a clockwise direction. The widths of the strips are the same as for block A; refer to the list on p.115 and the illustration above right.

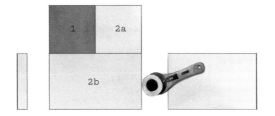

Assembly of quilt top

8 Sew one block B to the left-hand edge of one block A with a 5 mm (¼ in.) seam allowance. Press the seam open. **Note:** *The blocks are joined along the edges of the 16a pieces.* Repeat with the remaining blocks.

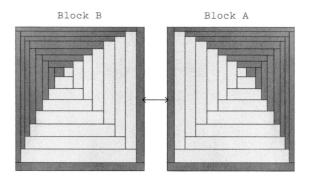

Block B   Block A

9 Sew the two pairs of blocks together along the edges of the 16b pieces. This will create a light circle in the quilt centre (see opposite). Press the seam open.

Finishing

10 Place your backing fabric, wrong side up, on a flat surface, securing the edges with masking tape. Place the wadding (batting) on top, and finally your completed quilt top. Use safety pins or tacking (basting) to secure the layers and avoid movement (see p.47, step 8).

11 Quilt the layers together by hand. Mark a straight line (with tailors' chalk or quilters' tape) diagonally from corner to corner of the quilt. Following that line, quilt the layers together by hand. Quilt further lines parallel to this one, approx. 2.5 cm (1 in.) apart to start with, increasing to 5 cm (2 in.) Use quilting threads in different contrasting colours. Sew towards yourself, with the non-sewing hand on the back of the quilt. Push the needle down and, as soon as you feel it through your quilt, rock it away from you and back up to the top. The stitches will be bigger on the top of the quilt than on the back.

12 Add binding, following the instructions on pp.78-79, but using strips 13.5 cm (5¼ in.) wide and a 2 cm (¾ in.) seam allowance for a chunkier binding.

Hand-quilt straight lines diagonally across the pieced quilt top.

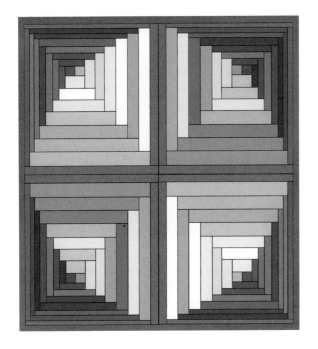

Now try...

A monochrome version of this quilt. Replace the colourful scraps and fabric remnants with dark-grey, black and off-white organic cotton for a strikingly graphic and contemporary result.

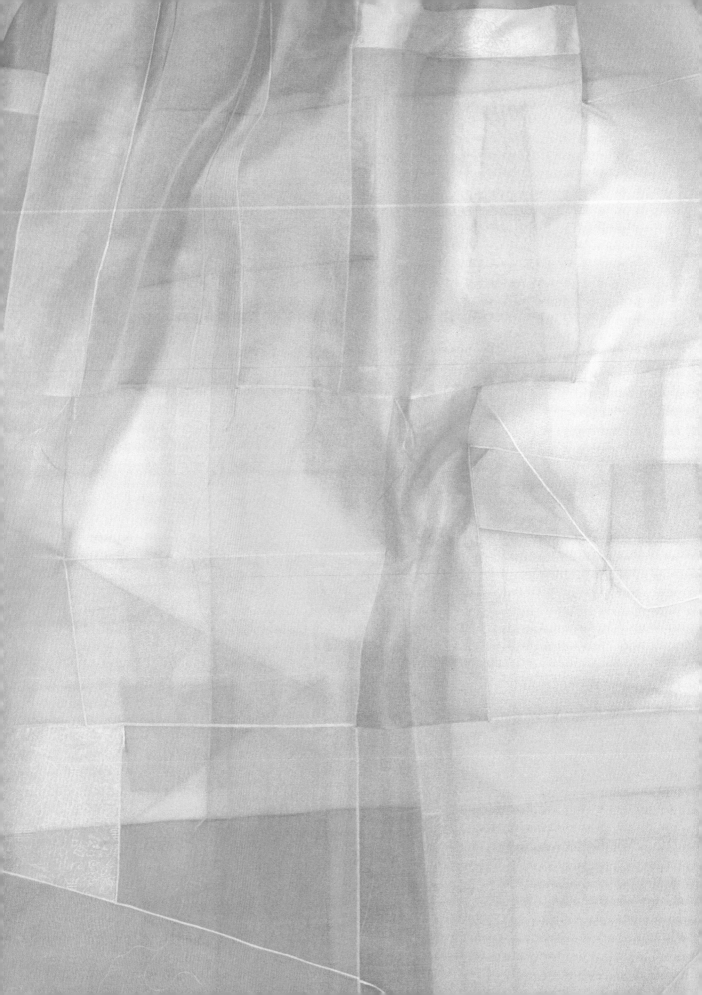

FREEFORM

Prior to the nineteenth century, 'crazy' patchwork in the West was a thrift craft and the product of poverty. Many different fabrics – wool, flannel, cotton and linen – could be combined to make a quilt that was entirely utilitarian, simply a means of keeping warm; unsurprisingly, very few examples have survived. Across the world, non-geometric, improvisatory patchwork typically has its origins in thrift and domestic economy, though the line between purely functional and aesthetic, even sentimental, object is inevitably blurred. It is thought that the 1876 display of Japanese *yosegire* textiles – sewn together from precious, salvaged fragments – at Philadelphia's Centennial Exposition inspired the Western craze for crazy patchworking as a leisure activity.

Chunghie Lee, skirt (detail), 2001
Machine-stitched silk gauze patchwork, 117 x 180 cm (46 x 70⅞ in.)
V&A: FE.137–2002

PATCHWORK

JOGAKBO

The term *jogakbo* (also *chogakpo*) refers to traditional
Korean wrapping cloths (called *bojagi* or *pojagi*) made
by patching scraps of fabric together into larger squares
or rectangles. A range of fabrics, from cotton and silk
to ramie, hemp and even paper – sometimes opaque and
sometimes light and translucent – is used in traditional
jogakbo-making, though one cloth is usually only made
from one kind of fabric. The scraps are sewn together
using a triple-stitched seaming technique known as
gekki, which results in a sealed, flat seam and gives
the wrappers their distinctive 'window pane' appearance.
Patches are joined into squares and the square form then
extended in an irregular, improvisatory fashion until
a cloth reaches the required size.

Steeped in tradition

Traditionally, Korean women, living in a male-dominated
society and excluded from formal education, concentrated
on domestic tasks such as weaving and embroidery,
creating *bojagi* by collecting scraps of fabric left over
from making dresses and quilts. This technique flourished
during the Joseon Dynasty (1392-1910), although its
origins are much earlier, with examples surviving from
as early as the twelfth century. Early cloths were used
in a Buddhist context. Traditional cloths often exhibit
the *obangsaek* (five directional colours) of blue, yellow,
red, white and black, but contemporary examples are
seen in a range of colours. The Victoria and Albert Museum
collection also includes a beautiful single-colour piece
from the early twentieth century (V&A: FE.303-2011).

Chungie Lee, *jogakbo* shoes, 1992
Pieced silk gauze, 28 x 6.5 cm
(11 x 2½ in.)
V&A: FE:280:2-1995

***Bojagi* (wrapping cloth), late
19th-early 20th century**
Silk gauze with plain-weave and
weft-float patterning patchwork,
73 x 88.9 cm (28¾ x 35 in.)
Los Angeles County Museum of Art

Chunghie Lee, woman's ensemble, c.1993

Bold areas of block colour – the fuchsia-pink waistband and green, silk-gauze jacket front, for example – contrast, here, with colourful areas of patchwork executed in the traditional *jogakbo* style. Korean textile artist Chunghie Lee has applied the techniques closely associated with traditional wrapping cloths to forms of dress originating in pre-modern Korea: *baji* (or *paji*) – loose-cut, relaxed trousers; and the *jeogori* (or *chōgori*), a Korean jacket style recognizable by the plain collar, short body and curving sleeve shape. Note the subtly non-symmetrical design of the jacket and the striking interplay between opacity, in the characteristic triple seams of the piecing, and the light, translucent silk gauze.

Pieced silk gauze, trousers: 127 x 44.2 cm (50 x 17⅜ in.)
and jacket: 42.5 x 150 cm (16¾ x 59 in.)
V&A: FE:281:1-2–1995

CUSHION WRAP

This project uses lightweight linen, similar to the ramie traditionally used for *jogakbo*, and borrows from the idea of the wrapping cloth, with silk ties added to create a cushion wrap – a twist on the more familiar zip-up cushion cover. Hand-stitching will give you seams that are strong and completely reversible, but you can also machine-stitch your pieces together. You can easily adapt the design for other cushion sizes, or even come up with your own. Once you have mastered the seaming technique, it can be easier (and more authentic) to improvise than to follow intricate piecing patterns.

You will need

Lightweight linen or ramie fabric. We recommend using five colours: a pale, medium, and a dark shade of one colour, and two contrasting colours:
Pale blue-grey, 50 x 50 cm (20 x 20 in.) and 63 x 32 cm (25 x 12 in.)
Mid-tone/cornflower blue, 30 x 20 cm (12 x 8 in.)
Dark navy blue, 30 x 20 cm (12 x 8 in.)
Pink, 30 x 20 cm (12 x 8 in.)
Lemon yellow, 30 x 20 cm (12 x 8 in.)

Lightweight Habotai silk to match the pink and yellow linens, 76 x 25 cm (30 x 10 in.) of each (you can also cover the cushion pad in Habotai silk of your choice if you wish – this pad requires a piece 45 x 90 cm/18 x 36 in.)

Cushion pad (pillow form), 41 x 41 cm (16 x 16 in.)

If hand-sewing, DMC Pearl Cotton, no.8, blue (334). (If you are planning to machine-stitch, choose a sewing thread to match the main blue-grey fabric colour.)

Tacking (basting) thread

Hand-sewing thread, to match the two silk colours

Hand-sewing needle

Dressmaking scissors

Long ruler

Optional

Hera (see p.11)

Cutting mat

Rotary cutter

Project by Caroline Gladstone

How to make

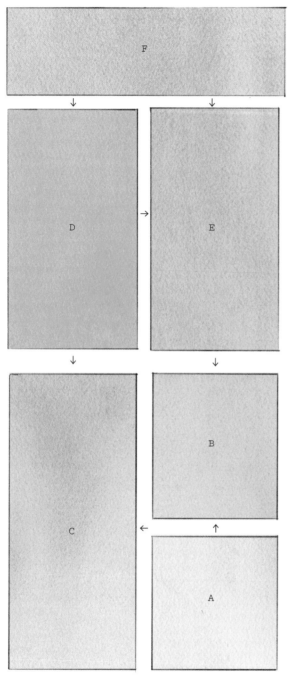

A joins to **B** / **AB** joins to **C** / **D** joins to
E / **DE** joins to **CB** / **F** joins to **DE**

1 First, measure diagonally across your
cushion pad, corner to corner. The final,
pieced square will need to be this tall and
wide. Our cushion measures 59 cm (23½ in.)
diagonally, so needs a 59 x 59 cm pieced
square.

2 Join pieces by hand or machine using
the instructions opposite and on p.128,
following the chart provided (see p.131).
Start by cutting out all the relevant
fabric shapes using the piece 4 template
on p.130 and the measurements given on
p.131. Some pieces on the chart are small
snippets, for which no template is provided
– use the chart, and your main pieces, as
a guide to cut the relevant shapes, adding
5 mm (¼ in.) seam allowances as required.
When using piece 4, join two pieces along
the diagonal line, being careful not to
allow this to stretch, as it is on the
bias. **Note:** *Some pieces, once joined,
will need to be trimmed to fit with their
'partners'. Any of the pieces can themselves
be pieced should you be short of fabric.*

3 Consult the illustration left for
a sample stitching order. Join pieces
together to form square or rectangular
blocks, as shown on the chart on p.131,
and then join these blocks together,
straight edge to straight edge. You can
join pieces in any order, but you can only
join in straight lines.

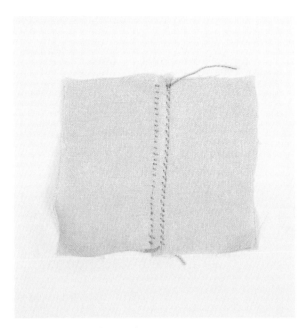

Hand-stitched linen pieces

Stitching by hand

1 Using the hera, or the back of a scissor blade, mark 5 mm (¼ in.) from the edge of one piece of fabric and 1 cm (⅜ in.) from the edge of the other. Marking with the hera (or blade) is like scoring paper – it leaves a clear crease line. Fold each piece along the crease line, and place the two together with the raw, folded edges inside.

2 Whip stitch (see p.17) the two pieces together along the fold. Just catch a few threads at the top of the fold and don't pull your thread too tight, as you will be opening the seam out flat. **Note:** *The DMC Pearl Cotton thread suggested here is intended to be a few shades darker than your fabric, for effect. You could also use ordinary hand-sewing thread in a matching shade, making the stitching much less visible.*

3 Open the pieces out flat with both seam allowances laying to one side, and fold the longer allowance down over the shorter – press this as flat as you can. Now fold the enclosed seam away from the stitch line, to conceal all raw edges.

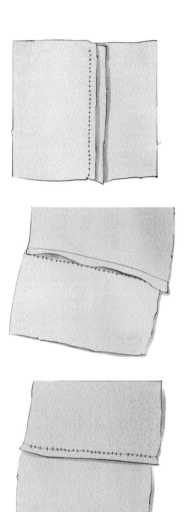

4 Now, using the unsewn edge of the folded seam as a guide, press the 'underneath' fabric piece back on itself, giving you another double fold to stitch along, as before. When you open this seam out, there will be two parallel lines of stitching visible: one with small, straight stitches, and one with longer, slanted stitches.

Stitching by machine

1 Using the hera, or the back of a scissor blade, mark 5 mm (¼ in.) from the edge of one piece of fabric, to form a crease line. Line up the raw edge of the second piece of fabric with this crease, and tack (baste) the two pieces together, with stitches close to the crease line.

2 Mark a second line, 5 mm below the first. Machine-stitch along this line and remove the tacking.

3 Fold the longer edge down over the shorter edge and then fold the whole enclosed seam over again, so that all raw edges are concealed. Machine-stitch the seam down, stitching close to the fold.

5 When your pieced square is finished, press and measure it. If you are following the chart, add the border now. If you are making your own design or a cover for a larger cushion pad, you can add a bigger border or more pieces. This is the beauty of this method – it grows organically!

6 To make the border, cut four pieces of pale-blue linen fabric, each 63 x 8 cm (25 x 3⅛ in.). Join them to the main square in the order shown above right, using the same method outlined above. Trim strips 1 and 2 to the width of the pieced panel before attaching strips 3 and 4.

7 Trim to the finished size required, plus 1.5 cm (⅝ in.) on each side for the hem. Mark the seam allowance line with a hera or scissor blade.

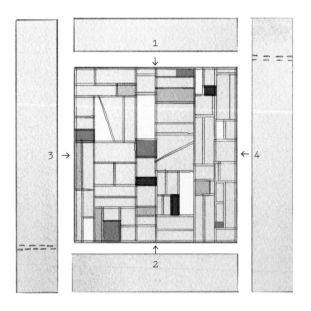

8 To hem the edges, fold the raw edge to the marked line on the 'front' of the square, then fold over again. Fold this hem back on itself (i.e., to the back of the square), giving you another double fold to whip stitch. Press.

9 Now make the cushion ties – two pink and two yellow (or colours of your choice). For each, cut a piece of silk measuring 50 x 10 cm (20 x 2 in.) Fold each lengthwise, right sides together, and stitch a 1 cm (⅜ in.) seam. Stitch across one end diagonally and trim away surplus fabric before turning the tie the right side out. Press.

10 Trace off the template for the corner pieces (see p.130), and cut two in pink silk and two in yellow silk. These corner pieces hide the joins and raw ends of the ties, ensuring a neat finish.

11 Position the ties made in step 9 over the corners on the back of the cover (place matching colours at opposite corners). Hand stitch each one in position, sewing only through one layer of the hem, so that no stitching is visible on the front. Turn the cover over and **slip stitch** (see p.17) each tie along the corner edges to secure.

12 Turn under and tack (baste) the seam allowances of each silk corner piece. Position each corner piece over a corner of the cover, concealing the tie, and slip stitch in place. Remove your tacking stitches.

The cushion ties knot elegantly at the back, creating a prominent design feature.

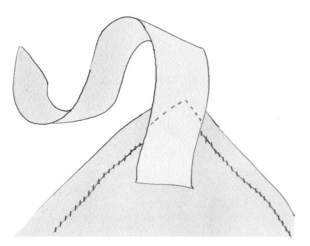

Now try...

Using different fabrics. A patchwork of thicker cotton fabric could be used as the front panel of a simple tote bag. Sheer or semi-sheer fabrics would make an attractive curtain panel to go in front of a small window.

Templates

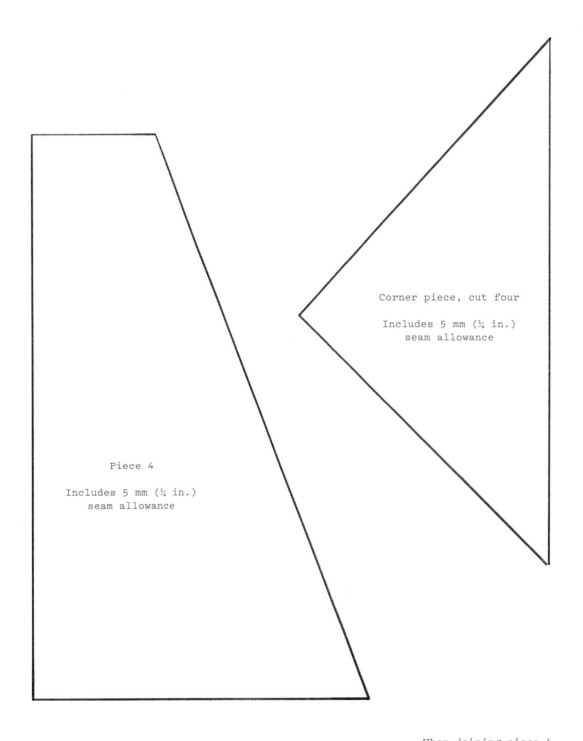

Corner piece, cut four

Includes 5 mm (¼ in.)
seam allowance

Piece 4

Includes 5 mm (¼ in.)
seam allowance

When joining piece 4,
join two together on
the diagonal seam, then
trim (if necessary)
to a rectangle before
joining to other pieces

Templates shown at 100%

Chart

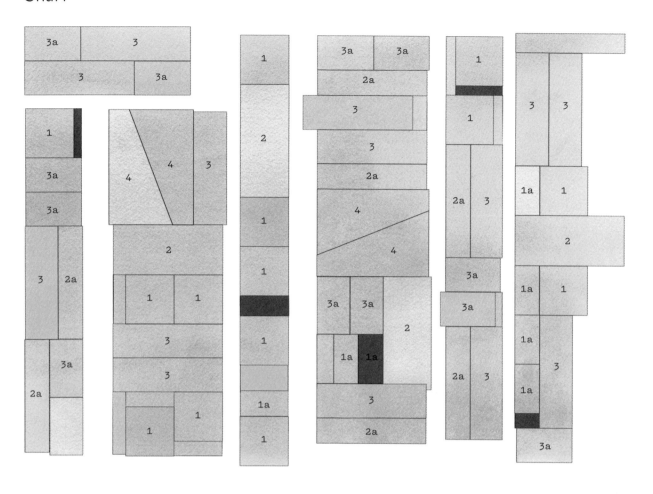

Main pieces

To replicate the design shown in the photograph on p.125, cut the following pieces and use the chart above to assemble them in rectangular blocks as shown. All measurements below include 5 mm (¼ in.) seam allowance. See also diagram on p.126.

1: 70 x 70 mm (2¾ x 2¾ in.)
1a: 40 x 70 mm (1⅝ x 2¾ in.)

2: 70 x 150 mm (2¾ x 5⅞ in.)
2a: 40 x 150 mm (1⅝ x 5⅞ in.)

3: 50 x 150 mm (2 x 5⅞ in.)
3a: 50 x 80 mm (2 x 3⅛ in.)

4: See template opposite

Filler pieces (snippets)

These are not numbered on the chart above. Once you have cut your main pieces, use the pieces and the chart above to cut these, remembering to add a 5 mm (¼ in.) seam allowance.

Note: *Some pieces, once joined, will need to be trimmed to fit with their 'partners. Any of the pieces can themselves be pieced should you be short of fabric.*

BORO

Derived from the Japanese *boroboro*, meaning something tattered or repaired, *boro* refers to the practice of reworking and repairing textiles (often clothes or bedding) through piecing, patching and stitching, in order to extend their use, in many cases far beyond their normal lifespans. It is associated with the indigo-dyed hemp clothing traditional in Japan before the introduction of cotton. Worn areas of cloth are patched over or older garments cut up and joined, with running stitches or areas of *sashiko* (see pp.20-29) used for reinforcement and to quilt layers of cloth together. This historical spirit informs the contemporary trend for 'distressed' or repaired-looking clothes; the exclusive FADE OUT (see pp.7-8) and Vetements denim labels, for example, arguably draw on the legacy of *boro*.

Thrift and creativity

In the nineteenth and early twentieth centuries, *boro* garments might be handed down through many generations of impoverished rural families, their making an expression of *mottainai* – a sense of regret concerning waste. An extreme example of patchwork's association with thrift, they are now recognized as a highly distinctive cultural product. Today, *boro* textiles, often futon covers, are regarded as works of art and a cultural record of homespun cloths, dyes and techniques. It is notable that the most heavily patched side of a *boro* panel, prized for its spontaneous and abstract qualities today, is often the back or inside of the piece, as more care was taken to arrange fabrics on the side that would be seen.

Japanese work jacket (detail, inside), early 20th century
90 x 120 cm (35⅜ x 47¼ in.)
Private collection

***Boro* fragment, probably originally part of a futon cover (detail, reverse), early 20th century**
110 x 55 cm (43¼ x 21⅝ in.)
Private collection

Robe, 1850–1900

All of the cotton fabric used to make this garment had a previous life and was recycled to make this piece of clothing. The result is a simple robe that looks curiously contemporary to modern eyes, accustomed as we are to seeing more luxurious versions of this type of garment – kimono that have been richly dyed or embroidered. Note the 'triangular' sleeves, which are common in traditional Japanese workwear.

Pieced and quilted cotton, 115 x 120 cm (45¼ x 47¼ in.)
V&A: FE.27–2015

BORO BAG

Many old *boro* robes have been patched and patched again, with the random stitches and areas of fabric wear giving them an incredible texture, which is prized by collectors. The improvisational effect of the patches has been compared to abstract art. This strong, unlined *boro* bag will withstand heavy use. It is covered in patches hand-sewn onto a foundation fabric. More patches can be added as it begins to take on the patina of use. Make it from new or recycled fabrics. *Boro* is a great technique for beginners to patchwork and quilting.

You will need

Striped or plain cotton fabric:
Bag handles: two pieces, each 11.5 x 35.5 cm (4½ x 14 in.)
Bag foundation: 38 x 95 cm (15 x 37½ in.)
Note: *Narrow-width Japanese striped kimono cotton was used for this bag, and the selvedges left on the sides of the cut panel. If you are using other fabric, add 1.5 cm (½ in.) to each long edge and press a hem, as for the short ends (see step 2).*

Assorted fabric scraps for *boro* patching, including plain, striped and woven patterns. (The quantity will depend on how you arrange your scraps. This is a good technique for fabrics that are slightly too thick for patchwork or have a slightly lower thread count, such as linen and cotton blends, lightweight denim, etc.)

One 100 m skein *sashiko* thread, Olympus medium, white

General sewing thread, dark grey or blue (or to match fabric scraps), to assemble bag

Sashiko needle, suitable for medium *sashiko* thread

Hand-sewing needle

Pins

Optional
Sewing machine

Project by Susan Briscoe

How to make

1 Start by making the bag handles, using your two 11.5 x 35.5 cm (4½ x 14 in.) pieces. Fold and press each handle as shown in the illustration below. Using *sashiko* thread, hand stitch along each long edge of each handle, going through all the layers, about 2 mm (¹⁄₁₆ in.) from the edge. Add another two rows of stitching along the length of the handle, for reinforcement.

2 At each short end of the foundation fabric, fold a 1.5 cm (½ in.) hem towards what will be the outside of the bag. There is no need to stitch this hem in place, as it will be covered with fabric patches and sewn down as you make your *boro*. If you are not using narrow-width traditional Japanese fabric, you will also need to do this along each long edge of the foundation fabric.

3 Start covering the foundation fabric with patches, working from the centre, as shown in the illustration opposite; this area will become the bottom of your bag. While there is no real rule to positioning the patches in *boro*, working 'outwards' in this way will make the patches overlap like shingles (tiles). Pin the first patches in place. **Note:** *Your patches do not have to be square or rectangular, but most old Japanese boro have mainly rectangular shapes, due to the fabrics having been recycled from kimono and other garments with minimal shaping.*

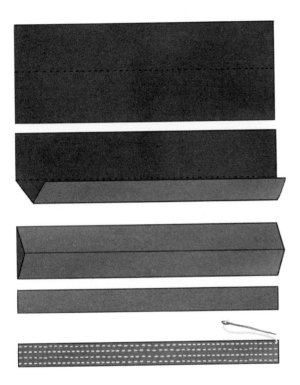

4 Add more patches, overlapping the previous, varying size, colours and patterns for effect. Begin stitching down the edges of the patches with uneven **running stitches** (see p.17), using your *sashiko* needle and thread. Start and finish your sewing with a knot, tucked under the edge of a patch. Your stitching lines do not have to be straight – many old *boro* have very wobbly lines – but you could follow stripes or stitch parallel to the patch edges. Continue adding patches, gradually covering all but the short ends of the foundation fabric – any raw edges at the sides of the bag will be hidden later, when the bag is finished. **Note:** *Take care not to accidentally cover any pins so you can't remove them later!*

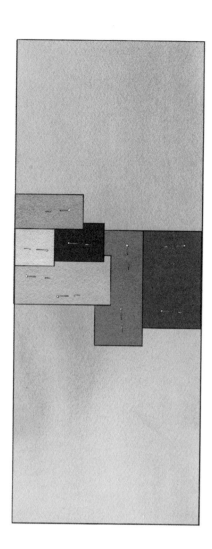
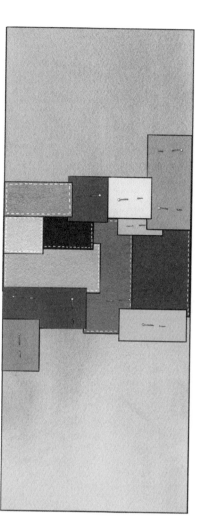

5 Position the bag handles at the ends
of the foundation fabric (these will become
the top edges of the bag), as shown in the
illustration above. The handles are sewn
onto the right side and more patches are
used to cover the handle ends. Make sure
the handles are centred at the 'tops' of
the bag, with the ends overlapping the edge
of the bag panel by 2.5 cm (1 in.). The gap
between the handle ends is 9 cm (3½ in.)
on each side. Make sure the handles are
the same length, in the same position on
each side of the bag, and not twisted. Use
several lines of running stitches going
back and forth to secure the handles in
place. Like all the *boro* stitching, this
will be visible inside the finished bag.

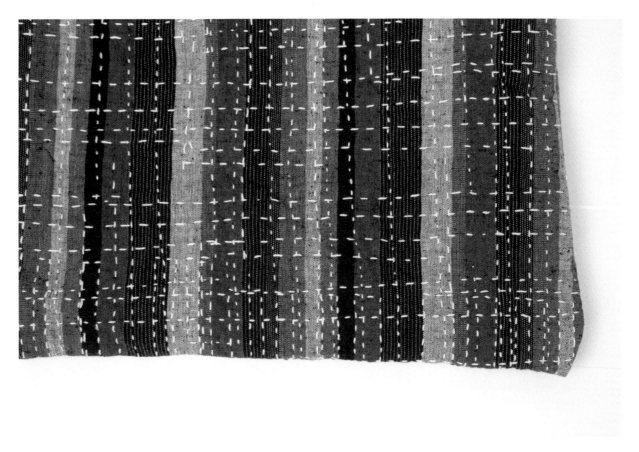

Extra stitching lines at the bottom of the bag - pictured here on the interior - provide added strength and durability.

6 Finish adding the *boro* patches to each end of the foundation fabric. When adding the final (top) row of patches, turn a 1.5 cm (½ in.) hem allowance under on each patch, unless you want to have a raw edge at the top of your bag.

7 Now start adding extra lines of running stitch, both horizontal and vertical, all over the bag panel. The lines don't have to go all the way across but they should be fairly close together, between 1 cm (⅜ in.) and 2.5 cm (1 in.) apart). When stitching at right angles over the edge of a patch, try to make your last stitch into the edge of the patch piece, as this will hold the raw edge in place and prevent too much fraying. After stitching all over, turn your *boro* panel over and add some extra stitching lines where the bottom of the bag will be, as extra reinforcement (as shown above). If you have used striped fabric for your panel, you can use the stripes to line up this stitching - a nice contrast to the more irregular stitching on the outside of the bag.

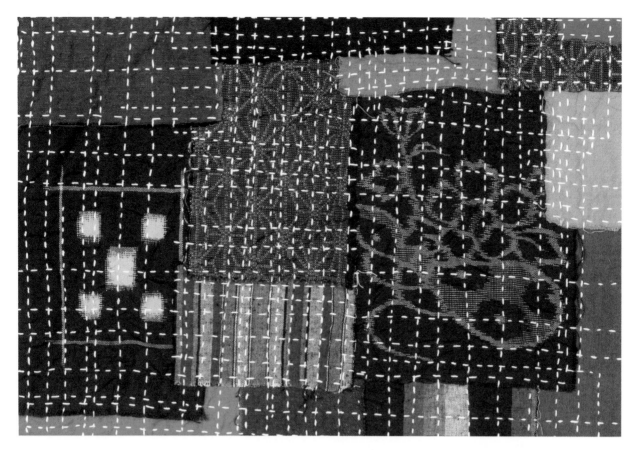

Your finished bag will showcase all your scrap fabrics, with the all-over stitching a unifying design feature.

8   Now it's time to construct your bag. Fold the *boro* bag panel in half, wrong sides (i.e., foundation fabric) together. Join the sides of the bag using dark general sewing thread, stitching about 3 mm (⅛ in.) from the bag edges. If hand sewing, use **backstitch** (see p.17). If sewing by machine, take a few reverse stitches at each end of the seam to secure. Now, using *sashiko* thread again, oversew up and down each side of the bag, sewing over the previous stitching line, so that it is hidden. Use two rows of oversewing, to create 'X' stitches on each seam.

9   Optional: Turn the bag inside out and add a small reinforcing patch running across the top of each of the side seams, stitching from the inside. To give the bag an authentic used look, machine wash at 40-60ºC. This will slightly wrinkle the *boro* and help to 'set' the running stitches.

Now try...

Changing the size of your bag. You can make this bag to any size by altering the size of your foundation fabric, which itself can be pieced, if you don't want to buy new. These textiles simply become more beautiful as they are used and worn, so are perfect for things that will have a tough life!

APPLIQUÉ

Appliqué is an ancient needlework technique, used as an embellishment, whereby smaller pieces of fabric are attached to the surface of base cloths; small pieces of rare or precious fabrics, especially, can be preserved in this way. The technique finds hugely varied and specific expression worldwide, from the bold katab-work of Saurashtra, Gujarat, to the embroidery-embellished appliqués of Pipli, in the east-Indian state of Odisha. Appliqué work was done by men in seventeenth-century Cairo, while Broderie Persé was popular in eighteenth-century Britain and America, the application of cut-out printed motifs to a base fabric giving an effect somewhat similar to that of Indian chintz. African-American 'story quilts' depicting Biblical themes – for example, the work of nineteenth-century quiltmaker Harriet Powers – also employ appliqué extensively.

Cover (detail), 1856–69
Embroidered wool and silk intarsia with wool and silk appliqué,
267 x 229 cm (105⅛ x 90⅛ in.)
V&A: CIRC.114–1962

HAWAIIAN APPLIQUÉ

The *tivaivai* quilt is specific to Hawaii, Tahiti and the Cook Islands, and to their diaspora. Today, there are three types of *tivaivai*: the pieced or *taorei* quilt is characteristic of Tahiti and the Cook Islands. Originating in the Cook Islands, the *ta taura* form uses floral motifs appliquéd to a contrasting-coloured background, in a symmetrical design. The third type is the *manu* or cut-out *tivaivai*. Here, the fabric is folded into sections, the design drawn on and cut out like a paper snowflake, before being sewn onto a base fabric.

History of the *tivaivai*

Before the arrival of Europeans in the sixteenth century, there was no woven cloth on the Pacific islands of Fiji, Papua New Guinea, Hawaii, the Cook islands and Tahiti; instead, islanders made a felt-textured fabric called *tapa* from the inner bark of mulberry and breadfruit saplings. Designs were painted or stamped onto the *tapa* (and these are considered to be the forerunner of the appliqués found on *tivaivai*). It is uncertain when quilting began in the Pacific, but it is generally accepted that it was primarily learned through contact with Euro-American culture; it is thought that the techniques came from the women who travelled to Tahiti on board *HMS Duff* in 1797. Once introduced, the techniques, patterns and motifs spread and were adapted throughout the islands of Polynesia, though quilting never supplanted the use of tapa and mats in Samoa and Tonga.

Na Wai O Maunaolu
(The Waters of Maunaolu),
Hawaiian quilt, 1900-30
Cotton, 199.4 x 190.5 cm
(78½ x 75 in.)
Shelburne Museum, Vermont

Queen Kapi'olani's Fan Quilt, early 20th century

The central 'feather and fan' motif on this large-scale quilt consists, remarkably, of a single piece of red fabric appliqué, stitched to the white base cloth. It is a traditional Hawaiian pattern, with the fans representing those of Queen Consort Kapi'olani (1834–99) and the feathers a reference to her royal coat of arms, which is supported by warriors bearing feather plumes. The border (also appliqué) takes the form of a Hawaiian flower garland, a *Maile lei*. Close, hand-worked 'echo' or 'contour' quilting and thick wadding give the quilt a three-dimensional quality.

Cotton, 191 x 221 cm (75¼ x 87 in.)
The American Museum in Britain: 1972.157

APPLIQUÉ BLOCK

Who can resist a cheery block in red and white? These colours are traditional in Hawaiian quilts, but of course you could use any two contrasting colours to make this block. Measuring approx. 32 x 32 cm (12½ x 12½ in.), it is the perfect size for a cushion top, or could be used as part of a larger wall hanging or quilt. The design is a simplified version of the stylized floral motifs that appear on Hawaiian quilts.

You will need

Quilting or dress-weight cotton in two contrasting colours, one piece of each, 35.5 x 35.5 cm (14 x 14 in.; one for background, one for appliqué)

General sewing thread, to match your appliqué fabric (red, in our project)

Quilting or appliqué needle, size 9 or 10

Plastic-coated freezer paper, min. 33 x 33 cm (13 x 13 in.) **Note:** *Do not confuse this with normal greaseproof/food-wrapping paper, which is non-adhesive!*

Stapler

Scissors, suitable for paper

Pencil

Appliqué pins

Embroidery, or other sharp, fine-pointed scissors

Project by Pippa Moss

How to make

1 Fold your freezer paper square in half, bottom edge to top, 'shiny' sides together. Fold into quarters, taking the left-hand edge over to the right-hand edge. Open these quarter folds back out, leaving a midline vertical crease in the half-square. Now take the bottom left-hand corner to the mid-point of the top edge of the half-square; repeat for the bottom right-hand corner. Then fold on the midline vertical crease, but this time so the undersides of the folded unit face each other, to create an 'accordion'.

4 Now unfold your paper and lay the labelled portion over your design template, matching the 'C' and 'E' labels. Trace the design carefully with a pencil and then carefully refold the paper.

5 Staple the paper in a few places, to keep it from shifting as you cut out the pattern shape. Cut along the marked line, then carefully remove the staples. Discard the unlabelled section and then open out your appliqué pattern.

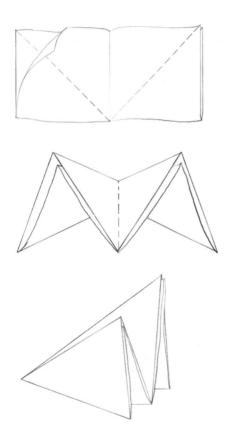

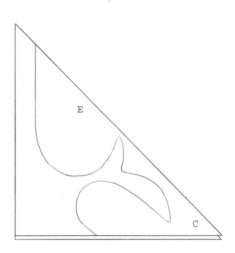

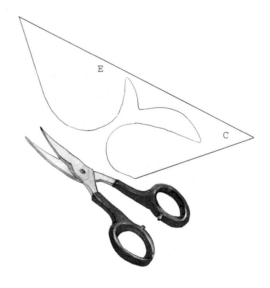

2 Orientate the folded paper in such a way as to match the design template on p.153. Mark a 'C' for 'centre' where all the paper folds meet, and 'E' for 'edge' along the long diagonal edge.

3 Photocopy or otherwise enlarge the design template on p.153 to full size, i.e. 100%.

6 Take your appliqué fabric (red in our photographs) and fold it in half diagonally, from corner to corner. Press and then do the same on the other diagonal. Repeat for the background fabric. The crease lines will aid in placement of the appliqué pattern.

7 Place your appliqué fabric onto the ironing board, right side up. The iron should now be set to cotton, no steam. Carefully flatten your freezer paper pattern (shiny side down) and centre it over the appliqué fabric, matching the paper folds with your fabric placement lines. Slowly 'heat baste' your freezer paper in place using the dry iron. Work from the centre outwards, keeping the paper pattern flat. If necessary, you can gently peel away and reposition the pattern. When done, flip the whole over and press again on the reverse, to ensure good adhesion.

8 Next, on a flat surface, position the appliqué piece directly on top of your background fabric, both right sides up and with the placement lines matching. Smooth and pin the appliqué piece in place, working from the centre outwards and using two or three pins for each part of the design. The pins will be gradually removed and the appliqué fabric trimmed as the work progresses.

9 A corner is a good place to start the appliqué. Work the appliqué from right to left if you are right-handed, and left to right if left-handed. First, taking care not to pierce the background fabric, cut through the appliqué fabric with your embroidery scissors, leaving an approx. 5 mm (³⁄₁₆ in.) seam allowance beyond the edge of your freezer paper pattern. Trim an area measuring only 5-8 cm (2-3 in.) at this point.

10 Next, thread your quilting or appliqué needle with a length of general sewing thread no longer than 46 cm (18 in.) and knot the end. Gather the work loosely in your non-dominant hand – the thumb and forefinger act as a clamp to hold the work in position while your dominant hand does the business of sewing! With the tip of your needle, sweep the seam allowance of the appliqué under the paper pattern, leaving a fold just proud of the paper edge. (This method of appliqué is known as 'needle-turn appliqué', because we use the needle to turn under the seam allowance).

11 Once the fold is secure and clamped between your thumb and forefinger, start the sewing by bringing the needle through from the back of the work, near the edge of a fold. Sew a series of small **whip stitches** (see p.17) along the fold to hold it in place, always working on the top of the cloth.

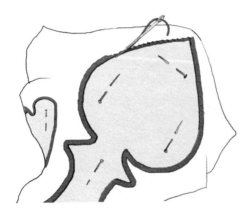

12 Continue to appliqué around the edge of the paper pattern piece. When the thread gets too short to work with, take it to the back and tie off with a knot. Trim the thread end and start again. **Tip:** *In difficult areas, like corners, stitches will need to be closer together, to hold down the fabric.*

Inner corners When working inner/concave corners, you will need to clip the seam allowance once, stopping the cut a thread or two short of the paper pattern. Work up to the cut, take an extra stitch and then fold the fabric after the cut and work the second part of the corner.

Points Again, work one side of the point, take a second stitch over the final stitch at the tip, trim any excess fabric then, with your needle tip, push the fold of cloth under until it reaches the seam that you have just sewn. Give the point a prod until it looks smooth, finger press and continue sewing to hold it in place.

Curves Inner/concave curves require some small clips in the seam allowance in order for the appliqué fabric to fold under neatly and smoothly. Outer or convex curves will not require clipping, but you can use your needle to smooth the seam allowance and prevent 'bumps' from appearing.

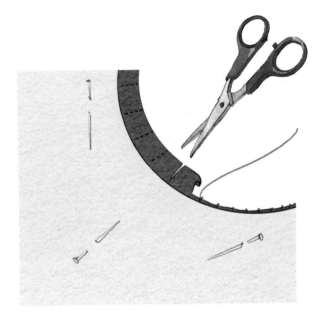

13 Once the appliqué is complete, remove all pins and peel off the freezer paper. Press the block from the reverse for a smooth finish.

Design template

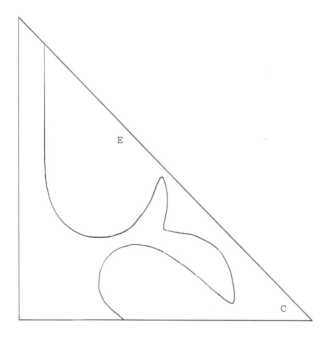

Template shown at 50%

Now try...

Your own design. It is fun to experiment with paper folding to create your own blocks; just remember to keep the shapes fairly simple and leave enough space between them for adequate seam allowances. Avoid very sharp thin points or very complex shapes. It is possible to make appliqué versions of people, animals, plants and flowers or just about anything! Use completed blocks for cushion panels, or sew them together to make a quilt top.

MOLA

The word *mola* can mean cloth, clothing or blouse,
although to many it has come to signify the stitched
panels made in the San Blas archipelago of Panama by
Kuna women. Traditional *mola* are made using a
combination of overlay, inlay and reverse appliqué,
though it is with the latter that they are most closely
associated. Most *molas* are made of two or three main
layers of fabric, dyed in bright colours. The first two
layers are laid on top of each other and the outline
of the main design is cut down, through the top layer,
turned under and stitched to the next layer to form
a channel. Subsequent layers can be added and small
pieces of different fabrics slotted between the layers,
to achieve a more intricate effect.

Mola characteristics

The first Mola Cooperative was formed in the 1960s
to unite artisans and promote their craft, and *mola*
are now commonly produced by Kuna women as a key source
of income. Inspiration for *mola* designs comes from
everyday life: flora, fauna, myths, religious beliefs
and rites of passage. Although needleworked clothing
was developing in the San Blas region from the 1800s,
the bright colours and intricate zoomorphic designs now
closely associated with *mola* were not commonly
used until the early 1900s.

The reverse appliqué of tribal groups from
Thailand is often confused with *mola*. Both consist
of designs created by channels cut in an overlay
fabric, but there the similarity ends. *Molas* are mainly
pictorial in nature, while the reverse appliqués of
South-East Asia are geometric; in Hmong appliqué, for
example, a design is generally precut into a folded
top layer of fabric before the layers are assembled,
establishing lines of symmetry and a near perfect
geometric pattern.

Mola fragment, mid-20th century
Cotton, 53 x 40 cm (20⅞ x 15¾ in.)
Private collection

Mola fragment, mid-20th century

Kuna traditional dress, from Panama, has not changed over the past hundred years. It consists of a wrap skirt and a blouse with puffed sleeves and peplum, made up using two similar, but not identical, *mola* panels. This is a fragment of such a panel, exhibiting saw-toothed cut edging on one of the fabric layers; it showcases the effect obtained when one layer of cloth is pieced from fabrics of many colours, so that these show through variously where the top layer of fabric is cut away. The effect is especially noticeable across this repeating, semi-geometric pattern.

Cotton, 48 x 42 cm (18⅞ x 16½ in.)
Private collection

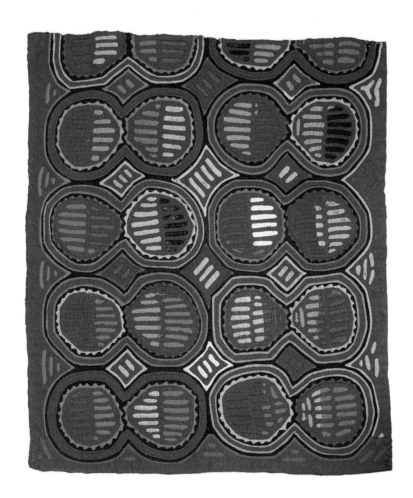

MINI BUCKET BAG

This little bag is a perfect introduction to the basic technique of *mola* – the decorative design is geometric, but you could apply the basic principles to a shape or motif of your choice. The effect is bold and intricate-seeming, but you only need a few basic stitches under your belt to get started!

You will need

Quilting cotton: burgundy and turquoise, one fat quarter of each (see p.12); pink, approx. 48 x 18 cm (19 x 7 in.; yellow, approx. 20 x 10 cm (8 x 4 in.)

Lightweight wadding (batting), approx. 33 x 49 cm (13 x 19¼ in.)

Sew-in craft interfacing, approx. 33 x 49 cm (13 x 19¼ in.)

General sewing thread, to match burgundy and turquoise fabrics

Tacking (basting) thread

Sharps needle, size 10

Embroidery, or other sharp, fine-pointed scissors

Sewing machine and thread

Machine needle suitable for heavyweight fabric

Optional

Dressmaker's carbon or transfer paper

Tailor's chalk, quilting pencil, or other erasable marker

Project by Caroline Craonie

How to make

1 Photocopy or otherwise enlarge the pattern pieces shown on p.163 to full size, i.e. 100%.

2 First make the decorated (outer) side of the bag – the piece with the *mola*. Start by cutting two patch pieces from each of the turquoise and yellow fabrics. (There is no need to transfer the spiral pattern.)

3 Cut a side piece from each of the burgundy and pink fabrics (remember to position the template on a fold, so that these pieces come out at twice the template length). Transfer the stitching lines and the four patch placement lines onto the wrong side of the pink piece. Then tack (baste) around each of the patch placement outlines.

4 Turn the pink piece right side up so that your markings are on the back. Tack the patches in place on the right side, alternating turquoise and yellow.

5 Place the burgundy piece, right side up, on top covering the patches, and then turn the whole project over, so that you can see the tacking around the patches on the pink side. Make another row of tacking through both layers, around each patch, approx. 2 mm (¹⁄₁₆ in.) outside the outer row of tacking. You should now have three rows of tacking visible on the pink side, and one on the burgundy.

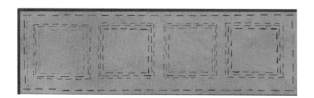

6 Now, working one patch at a time, use embroidery scissors to cut **the burgundy fabric only** just 2 mm (¹⁄₁₆ in.) outside the visible tacked line. Using the point of your needle, and burgundy thread, turn the raw outer edge of the burgundy fabric under, and stitch down with small **whip stitches** (see p.17), worked close together. The pink fabric will be exposed. **Tip:** *You may find it helpful to cut as you go, working a little way ahead of your stitching.*

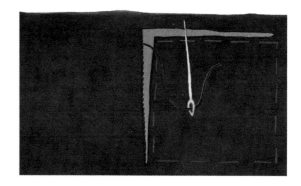

7 When you have stitched around the outer edge, turn under and stitch around the inner edge of the rectangle, removing the tacking as you go. Round off the corners slightly. You should now have four pink rectangle outlines on your side panel!

8 Now trace and transfer the spiral line of the patch template (p.163) into the centre of your first patch, using dressmaker's carbon paper or another method of your choice (see p.16 for full instruction). Tack the design through all fabric layers, NOT on the pattern line, but between the lines.

9 Cut along the design line, **through the burgundy fabric only.** Turn under the raw edges and stitch, as before, all round the design. You will find it easier to start at the outer edge and work inwards, and then spiral out again. This time, the yellow or turquoise of the patch underneath will be exposed. **Tip:** *To help the edges turn under, make two very tiny cuts at the start of your line.* Remove the tacking when the stitching is completed and repeat for the three remaining patches. Press.

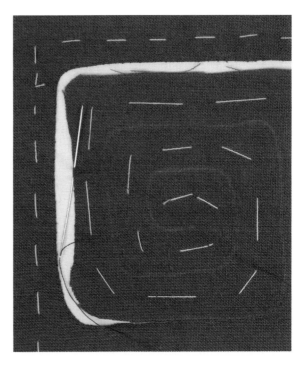

Transfer the spiral patch design shown p.163 and tack in place, as instructed in step 8.

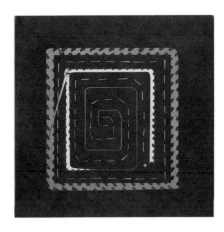

10 To make up the bag, first cut out one side, one base and one handle from each of the interfacing and wadding/batting (note the different cutting line for the handle). Cut one base and one handle from the burgundy fabric. Cut one base and one side from the turquoise fabric (to act as a lining).

11 Make a separate 'bag' out of each material, i.e. wadding, interfacing and turquoise fabric, taking care, on the interfacing and turquoise layers, to stitch along the lines marked in red on the templates. For each layer, first stitch the short (side) seam of the side piece, right sides together, to create a tube. Then stitch the base to the bottom of the tube. **Tip:** *You may need a heavyweight fabric needle in your machine to stitch the interfacing.* After stitching, trim away most of the seam allowance on the wadding and interfacing 'bags' and all of the seam allowance on their top edges. Turn the wadding and interfacing layers right side out. Leave the turquoise layer as stitched (i.e., wrong side out).

12 Now make the outer bag in the same way, using the burgundy 'mola' piece and the burgundy base. Turn right side out.

13 Now for assembly! Nest the wadding 'bag' inside the outer, burgundy 'bag'. Nest the interfacing 'bag' inside this. Turn the seam allowance at the top edge of the outer bag over the upper, raw edges of the wadding and interfacing to the inside of the bag. Tack in place.

14 To make the handle, start by folding the burgundy fabric piece in half lengthwise, right sides together, and stitch a seam along the long edge. Turn the tube right side out, and press flat, with the seam centre back.

15 Place the wadding handle piece on top of the interfacing handle piece, and then machine stitch down both long edges. To get this layer inside the fabric handle, fold in half lengthwise and push it inside the fabric tube, before opening it out flat.

16 Position the handle. With the handle seam on the underside, place the seam allowances of the short raw ends against the inter-facing layer inside the bag, with one short end centred over the bag's side seam. Pin or tack in place. Then machine stitch all around the top edge of the bag, through all of the layers, securing the handle and the seam allowance and neatening the top edge of the outer bag. You may need the heavyweight needle again.

17 Now nest the turquoise bag lining (wrong side out) inside the outer bag – wrong sides will now be facing each other, thus hiding all the exposed seams. Match up the side seams. Turn under the seam allowance at the top edge of the bag lining and then **slip stitch** (see p.17) in place to the outer bag.

Now try...

Scaling up! You could use the same pattern supplied here to create *mola* patches for decorating a much larger, plain bag. Once you've got the hang of it, the same technique can also be adapted to create any motif, including the zoomorphic designs typical of authentic *mola*!

Templates

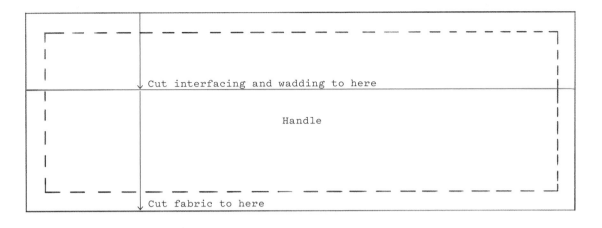

Cut interfacing and wadding to here

Handle

Cut fabric to here

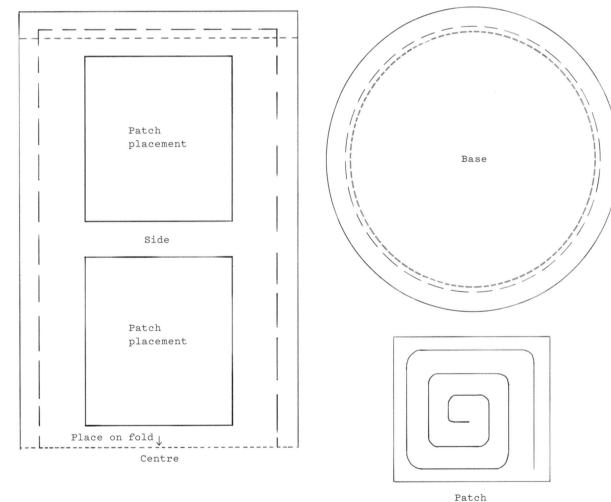

Patch
placement

Side

Patch
placement

Place on fold

Centre

Base

Patch

———————————— Cutting line

— — — — — — Stitching line

- - - - - - - Stitching line for interfacing and lining

Templates shown at 50%

INTARSIA

The origins of intarsia, or 'inlay', appliqué are to be found in Italy, Spain and the Middle East. It has been described as the technique that links true patchwork and appliqué. While applied designs are cut and stitched onto a background fabric, inlay involves the setting in of patterns into a perfectly cut background. The two elements are frequently cut at the same time to ensure a perfect fit and both sides of the work are alike. The pieces are generally sewn together with a darning stitch or a fine whip stitch, and the technique requires a non-fraying fabric.

Military precision

Inlay appliqué has been worked in a wide variety of materials in many different local contexts, including sixteenth-century France, Italy and Spain; Iran (where the city of Resht is particularly closely associated with inlay); and colonial Ghana. During the second half of the nineteenth century, a very particular type of inlay was being produced, mainly in Britain and almost exclusively by tailors. It was made from heavy, non-fraying uniform or suit cloth, embellished with embroidery, and was mainly figurative. This technique demanded a high degree of skill and artistry. The same uniform fabrics were also being used to produce the geometric patchwork of soldier's quilts.

Cover, 1856-69
Embroidered wool and silk intarsia with
wool and silk appliqué, 267 x 229 cm
(105⅛ x 90⅛ in.)
V&A: CIRC.114-1962

John Brayshaw, textile picture, c.1850
Wool intarsia with wool appliqué and
silk embroidery, 43 x 46.1 cm
(16⅞ x 18⅛ in.)
V&A: AP.27-1917

Cover or hanging, 1875–85

Said by its former owner to have been worked by a male ancestor while on a long sea voyage (though conservators at the Victoria and Albert Museum note that it shows evidence of two hands), this broadcloth cover depicts an A to Z of scenes, from 'Admiration' to 'Zingari' (an archaic Italian term once used in English to refer to the Romany community), worked in both traditional appliqué and intarsia. Fashionably dressed men and women – their clothing has been used as the basis for dating the quilt – engage in the various rituals of courtship. The presence of gaming motifs in the quilt border suggests that the quilt may have been created in relation to a card game, though it was also common in the period to draw a parallel between love and gambling.

Broadcloth with intarsia, appliqué in woven wools and silk velvets, and embroidery, 161.3 x 118 cm (63½ x 46½ in.)
V&A: T.200–1969

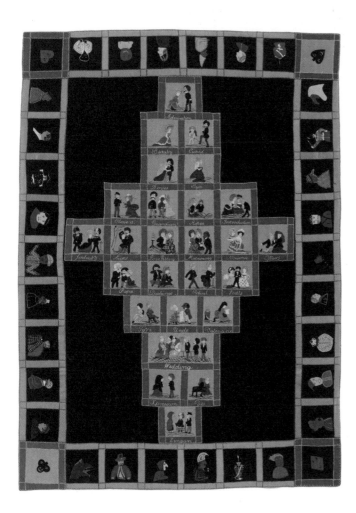

SOFT TOY

Using modern materials and a specially devised technique, it is possible to replicate the intricate 'inlay' patchwork used in quilts such as that shown on the previous page. The method is easy and economical, so that very little material goes to waste, even when working with complicated shapes such as the card suits shown here. If you intend this as a toy for a baby or toddler, take special care to make your stitching secure.

You will need

100% wool felt, a total of six pieces 9 x 9 cm (3½ x 3½ in.) minimum: two grey, two red, one blue and one white, plus an optional small amount of black
Scrap cotton fabric of any colour, approx. 24 x 24 cm (9½ x 9½ in.)
Fusible web, to match wool felt quantity
Hand-sewing thread, in colours matching your felt
Hand-sewing needle
Dressmaking scissors
Pen or pencil
Scissors, suitable for paper
Embroidery, or other sharp, fine-pointed scissors
Toy stuffing

Optional

Baking parchment
Rotary cutter
Cutting mat
Quilting ruler
Sewing machine

Project by Gillian Travis

How to make

1 Cut a total of six felt squares, each
9 x 9 cm (3½ x 3½ in.). Cut two squares
from each of two colours (red and grey)
and one square each from two colours
(blue and white). A rotary cutter, cutting
mat and ruler will make this easier, but
dress-making scissors will do just as well.

2 Cut six cotton squares, each 8 x 8 cm
(3 x 3 in.), i.e., 5 mm (¼ in.) smaller
all round than the felt squares. Cut six
fusible web squares the same size as the
cotton squares.

3 Using a sharp pencil, trace the club,
heart and spade templates shown opposite,
two of each, onto the paper side of the
fusible web, positioned centrally.

4 Referring to the manufacturer's
instructions, attach fusible web to the
felt squares, positioning centrally and
squarely and making sure you press the
paper side and not the glue side.

5 Using the point of your embroidery
scissors, poke a hole in the corner of
one of the traced shapes and carefully
cut it out. Repeat for all six squares,
making sure you cut through both the
fusible web and felt.

6 Remove the paper backing of the
fusible web from all of the felt shapes
and 'backgrounds'.

7 Place one background piece, glue side
up, on your ironing board and carefully
ease a felt shape of a different colour,
also glue side up, into the cut-out hole.
Position a cotton square centrally on
top. Referring to the manufacturer's
instructions, fuse the cotton square in
place. **Tip:** *You may need to use a sheet
of baking parchment over the fabric to
ensure no glue gets stuck to your iron!*

8 Repeat to make six squares, ensuring
that each shape is a different colour
to its background for maximum impact.

9 Using general thread that matches
the background colour, make small stitches
across the join between the shape and
the background, closing any gaps between
the two.

10 If you want to add faces to your shapes,
cut out eye and mouth shapes from small
scraps of black felt. Stitch these firmly
on to the shapes. Add extra features with
more felt pieces.

11 Press each of the squares and then join them together into the cube shape, as shown below. Start by placing two squares right sides together and **whip stitching** (see p.17) along one edge. Add the others as shown, and then begin to form the squares into a 3D cube shape. Over-sew the remaining seams, leaving one side open to allow for stuffing.

12 Fill the cube with stuffing, poking it right down into each corner, and then proceed to whip stitch the last edge closed.

Now try...

Making cubes in any size and with different combinations of colour, as shown in our photography. They make good pincushions or stress toys! For babies, you can add some interest by making the stuffing 'noisy' – wash and dry some crisp packets and add them to the stuffing, for a crunchy feel.

Design templates

Template shown at 100%

ABOUT THE MAKERS

Jenny Barlow

Jenny Barlow is a respected teacher in the world of patchwork and quilting. She has a wealth of knowledge and a large and interesting collection of quilts and other textiles, built up over a period of 30 years. Barlow has taught a wide range of techniques in an equally wide range of locations. She has been a member of the The Quilters' Guild of the British Isles since 1980. Among her particular interests are the wholecloth quilts from the North East of England. www.quilt-with-jenny.co.uk

Susan Briscoe

Susan Briscoe is a designer and textile artist, whose interest in sashiko began when she was teaching English in Japan. She now lives in Perthshire, Scotland, where she teaches patchwork and sashiko quilting, and writes and designs for patchwork and needlecraft magazines. She is author of, most recently, The Ultimate Sashiko Sourcebook: Patterns, Projects and Inspirations (2005) and Quilt Essentials: Japanese Style (2013), among many other practical books on patchwork and quilting. www.susanbriscoe.com

Caroline Crabtree

Caroline Crabtree was an apprentice at the Royal School of Needlework (RSN) before embarking a freelance career, in which she has pursued an increasing interest in global embroidery, costume and household textiles. Her first book, World Embroidery (1993), was followed by Patchwork, Appliqué and Quilting (2007) and Beadwork: A World Guide (2009), both co-authored. She (mostly) retired from travelling and teaching in 2002.

Jenny Haynes

Jenny Haynes (née Nilsson) learned pattern cutting and tailoring in her native Stockholm. Her passion for fabrics took her to London, where she studied fashion and textiles at the London College of Fashion. She went on to develop her own label Papper, Sax, Sten (Paper, Scissors, Stone). Her bespoke quilts and furnishings are recognized for their clean and simple design. In 2015, Haynes was invited by the Swedish Chamber of Commerce to contribute to Heal's Swedish Summer Exhibition. www.pappersaxsten.com

Florence Knapp

For over a decade, Florence Knapp has written the 'Flossie Teacakes' blog, on which she shares her adventures in quilting, dressmaking and the life that goes on in between her stitches. Knapp designs sewing patterns, occasionally writes for magazines and is working on her first book, about English paper piecing. She lives with her husband, two teenaged children and their dog, Nell. www.flossieteacakes.blogspot.com

Pippa Moss

Pippa Moss lives in Suffolk. Born in Princeton, NJ, she made several quilts with her twin sister and mother while still a teenager. Since coming back to quilting in 1989, she has made many quilts, as well as teaching and giving talks. Formerly a university lecturer in Environmental Science, Moss now works in accountancy. She is a member of the Quilters' Guild of the British Isles, and the British Quilt Study Group. Pippa is also a keen bellringer. www.welshquilts.blogspot.com

Ruth Singer

Ruth Singer is a contemporary textile artist inspired by heritage and textile traditions. She has been making professionally since 2005 and, before that, worked in museums including the V&A, London. In 2015, Singer was Artist in Residence at the National Centre for Craft & Design, Sleaford, and in 2016, was awarded the Fine Art Quilt Masters prize at the Festival of Quilts. In 2017 she was Artist in Residence at Leicester University Department of Genetics. She has written three sewing books and runs textile workshops around the UK. www.ruthsinger.com

Gillian Travis

An award-winning textile artist, author and tutor, Gillian Travis is also an avid traveller and most of the quilts she makes are inspired by her travels. Her passion for photography and a love of natural fabrics, bright colours and machine stitching have resulted in several collections of contemporary quilts, including recent work inspired by visits to Scandinavian countries. www.gilliantravis.co.uk

INDEX

Picture credits

7 above: courtesy Brigitte Kopp. Winner of Fine
Art Quilt Masters at The Festival of Quilts, 2014
7 below: Photo: Christophe Cake. Make-up artist:
Yeorg Kronnagel. Art director: Tobias Noventa.
Model: Yukiko Pica Yamane.
8 above: courtesy Kate Loudoun Shand.
Photo: ny-lon design Ltd
8 below: Photo: Patrick Jendrusch. Make-up artist:
Memo Schmage. Styling: Ivi Geist. Art director:
Tobias Model: Quila Lulu Anastasia.
9 above left: courtesy Estate of Charles James
9 above right: Catwalkpictures.com
61: courtesy Schiaparelli
92: Granger/Bridgeman Images
93: courtesy The American Museum in Britain, Bath
101: courtesy The Ah-Tah-Thi-Ki Museum,
Clewiston, Florida (ATTK Catalog No. 1996.55.4)
111: Los Angeles County Museum of Art, Gift
of The Betty Horton Collection (M.86.134.19)
121 below: Los Angeles County Museum of Art,
Costume Council Fund (AC1995.118.4)
133: courtesy Susan Briscoe
145: Shelburne Museum, Vermont/Bridgeman Images
146-47: courtesy The American Museum in
Britain, Bath
155, 156, 157: courtesy Caroline Crabtree

Acknowledgments

The publishers would like to thank Anne Williams,
who acted as technical editor for this book. Caroline
Crabtree and Christine Shaw kindly allowed the
re-use of historical text from *Quilting, Patchwork
& Appliqué: A World Guide* (2007).

Our thanks also go to the Victoria and Albert
Museum curators who read and advised on the
historical texts: Clare Browne, Sau Fong Chan,
Avalon Fotheringham, Anna Jackson, Rosalie Kim,
Divia Patel and Josephine Rout.

DMC threads are available from DMC stockists
throughout the UK and internationally. Please
visit www.dmccreative.co.uk or www.dmc.com
for more information.

We would love to see what you create! Share your
pictures online using the hashtag #vamMakers